IN THE
NAME
of
GOD

TIMOTHY DEMY
GARY P. STEWART

HARVEST HOUSE™ PUBLISHERS

EUGENE, OREGON

Cover by Koechel Peterson & Associates, Minneapolis, Minnesota

IN THE NAME OF GOD

Copyright © 2002 by Timothy J. Demy and Gary P. Stewart
Published by Harvest House Publishers
Eugene, Oregon 97402

Library of Congress Cataloging-in-Publication Data
Demy, Timothy J.
    In the name of God / Timothy J. Demy, Gary P. Stewart
      p. cm.
    Includes bibliographical references.
    ISBN 0-7369-1022-0
    1. Terrorism—Religious aspects—Christianity. 2. Terrrorism—Religious aspects. I. Stewart, Gary (Gary P.) II. Title

BT736.15 .D46 2002
303.6'25—dc21   2002017177

Printed in the United States of America

02   03   04   05   06   07   08   09   10   / BP-CF /   10   9   8   7   6   5   4   3   2   1

To American citizens and service members who gave their lives on September 11, 2001, and in Operation Enduring Freedom. We will not forget.

Acknowledgments

This book was written as our nation and the authors walked through the valley of the shadow of death. Beyond the headlines there were several personal traumas and tragedies experienced by the authors during the months of writing that made the completion of this work both difficult and essential. We have shed tears for family, friends, and loved ones in these days and have learned afresh the meaning of God's assurance, "My grace is sufficient for you."

Scripture tells us that as iron strengthens iron in the forging of weapons for war, so too does one friend strengthen another in the preparation for the battles of life. We have been blessed with several who have strengthened us spiritually, emotionally, and intellectually for this volume. Some of them have been essential to the book's completion even though they were unaware of its writing. Others prayed while we wrote, and yet others gave helpful comments through conversations and questions.

From Tim: Thank you Neff Blackmon, Randy Cash, Tom Grassey, Phil Gwaltney, Al Hill, Alan Keiran, and Marty Stahl. Each of you has been very personally involved in the events of September 11, 2001, and continue that service today. You have supported me, but more important, you have served our nation. To Lynn Barnes, who kept after me every day and provided articles, books, and "just one more thing to read"—thank you, soon it will be your turn. And to my wife, Lyn, who gave up evenings, holidays, and family time once again, thanks for your support and your red pen.

From Gary: Thank you Col. Douglas F. Ashton for your support and confidence. You have my greatest respect. Whenever I write, I think of J. Daryl Charles and the advice he has given me over the years. I value your friendship more than you will ever know. Thank you, Dr. Frank E. Young—with all your experience and expertise in medicine, government, and ministry, you have always treated me as an equal, though I certainly am not. Thank you, William F. Wood and Jason Madison, for your administrative assistance throughout this time. A special thanks goes to my children; it is an honor being your dad. Dad, thanks for serving America in the Second World War. I am honored to follow in your footsteps in this war on terrorism. Thank you to my wife, Kathie, for your encouragement and willingness to give up the holiday season with friends and family so this could be completed on time. There aren't enough words to express all you have done.

Dr. Jan Patterson gave significant guidance and medical expertise with information on biological and chemical terrorism. We are grateful to everyone at Harvest House who so enthusiastically supported us throughout the book's preparation. We especially thank our editor, Steve Miller, for his insights, guidance, and encouragement. And thank you to Bob Hawkins, Jr.,

Carolyn McCready, LaRae Weikert, Terry Glaspey, John Constance, and Julie McKinney for catching the vision for this to become a book.

This work is based entirely upon open-source information and unclassified material and it represents the research, analysis, and views solely of the authors. Nothing in these pages represents the position of the U.S. government, Department of Defense, the U.S. Navy, or the U.S. Marine Corps. Any factual errors are, regrettably, those of the authors.

The LORD is my light and my salvation;
whom shall I fear?
The LORD is the defense of my life;
whom shall I dread?

PSALM 27:1

"Our nation—this generation—will lift the dark
threat of violence from our people and our future.
We will rally the world to this cause by our efforts
and our courage. We will not tire, we will not falter,
we will not fail."

PRESIDENT GEORGE W. BUSH
Address to the United States
September 20, 2001

Contents

Getting a Clear Focus

The catalyst for this book was clearly the terrible and tragic events of September 11, 2001, but the book's inception was in the mid-1990s. Like all Americans, we were shocked and angered by the events that took place on September 11, 2001. But unlike many people, we were not surprised. For the last several years we have studied and discussed terrorism personally and professionally in both public and private forums. The convergence of religion, terrorism, war, and international relations is something that has gradually been moving from the back page to the front page in newspapers around the world. Issues of faith and force, religion and warfare, are now a daily occurrence. What we offer in the following pages is a portion of that with which we have wrestled and watched for a long time.

Nearly a decade ago we stood together in New York City looking up at the twin towers of the World Trade Center, marveling at their magnificence and magnitude. We were attending a professional conference and the evenings provided much-needed time to reflect on what we believed and how we might best communicate those beliefs to others. As we walked the nearby streets, we talked about topics pertaining to faith and force. We talked about war and peace, justice and compassion, love and hatred. We had both seen and experienced a great deal in our years of military service as officers and chaplains. As we talked, our friendship grew and we found our resolve and our hope strengthened.

Now, years later, in a new decade, a new century, and a new millennium the return trip to New York City is for a different purpose and the sights are not the same. Standing in the same location, one looks down rather than up. Walking the same streets is not done with the carefree attitude of years past. It is a city of life, but also a city of death. And though the circumstances have changed, the concerns have not.

As Christians, chaplains, citizens, and friends, we are further down the road on which God has placed us, but the discussions are no different. Justice, war, love, hatred, and terrorism are more a part of our lives than previously. What is different is that this time, tears rather than bright lights blur the sights. Our emotions are not those of fear but of resolve.

These are crucial days in the life of our world, and the months and years ahead will be no less important. We believe that terrorism is not a short-term crisis, but a long-term concern. The war against terrorism will not be short. Therefore it is important that Christians understand what terrorism is, what motivations drive it, how dangerous it has become, and why it must be destroyed. Ultimately, there are only two responses to terrorism. We can apply our beliefs to the problem and address it from the perspective of faith, or we can be influenced by the beliefs of others and succumb to fear. Properly understanding terrorism and bringing our faith to bear against it will provide us with the courage and commitment to pursue a just cause and its necessary end.

Our interest is primarily in religiously motivated terrorism because we believe that the blood that will be spilled by tomorrow's terrorist murderers and martyrs will flow because they believe God wants it to be done. They are sincere, but they are wrong—dead wrong.

Terror Takes Its Toll

Remembering a Horrible and Historic Day

> The American people are responsible for the actions of their government and they must question all of the crimes that their government is committing against other people. Or they—Americans—will be targets of our operations.... Next time it will be very precise and [the] WTC will continue to be one of our targets in the U.S. unless our demands are met.[1]
>
> **Nidal Ayyad**
> *Conspirator in the bombing*
> *of the World Trade Center, February 1993*

The world has changed and will never be the same again. The saying "you can't go back" has never been more accurate and certain. The facts of September 11, 2001 are clear: four airplanes, thousands dead and injured, the World Trade Center, the Pentagon, New York City, Washington, D.C.,

the Pennsylvania countryside. It is a day that will be remembered the rest of our lives. The facts are clear, but they don't
answer all the questions. Who is responsible? Why such
hatred? Could something have been done? Will it happen
again? Who are they? What do they want? What should we do
next as individuals, as a nation, or even globally?

It is in the hearts and minds of men and women that the
ideas of terrorism, religiously motivated and otherwise, begin.
And motivations are rarely pure and simple. The actions of our
hands flow from the attitudes of our hearts. The photographs of
the events of September 11 are clear and vivid, but the histories
and beliefs that caused the events are complex and confusing.

Oddly enough, the words cited at the beginning of this
chapter are the words of a naturalized U.S. citizen who gradu-
ated from Rutgers University and worked as a chemical engi-
neer for a New Jersey company. He was one of five terrorists
who orchestrated and carried out an attack on the World Trade
Center that killed six people and injured more than a thousand
nearly a decade ago. Was he an unlikely terrorist who "risked a
good life in America by participating in the plot"?[2] No, he was
the perfect terrorist, one whose loyalty to an extremist form of
Islam and unbridled hatred for democratic America never
wavered. Though he may have appeared to be a loyal citizen,
he wasn't, which is made clear by his two-time use of the word
"our" in the quotation above.

We must not equate citizenship with security. Radical Islamists (or any others) who immigrate to the United States have no
interest in becoming loyal American citizens. Historically,
Muslims do not identify themselves by ethnicity or territory,
nor do they refer to non-Muslims in such terms. Non-Muslims
are referred to as infidels (*kafir*). Muslims desire to be Muslim
above everything else. "Muslims tend to see not a nation subdivided into religious groups but a religion subdivided into
nations."[3] The modern national boundaries of the Middle East
are, to many Muslims, nothing more than the divisions of

Islamic lands imposed by western imperialists after the fall of the Ottoman Empire in 1918.[4] For Muslims, the common religious belief in the redemptive power of a single and unified Islamic community (*umma* or *ummah*)[5] keeps them loyal and closely tied to their Islamic roots in the Middle East no matter where they live. Therefore, it should not be surprising that the first three British casualties of the war against terrorism in Afghanistan were Muslims fighting *for* the Taliban.[6]

Democracy vs. Terror

Ayyad was right about one thing: we are responsible for the decisions of our government. The U.S. Constitution clearly reminds us of this responsibility:

> *We the people* of the United States, in order to form a more perfect Union, establish justice, insure domestic tranquility, provide for the common defense, promote the general welfare, and secure the blessings of liberty to ourselves and our posterity....

In order to unite, not perfectly but *more* perfectly, we have been afforded the privilege and responsibility to vote for our leaders. We do this by choice or by default—that is, we affect the outcome of an election whether or not we go to a voting booth. Therefore, as American citizens, we are ultimately responsible for the decisions our representatives make. For this reason we are also responsible to support them or *legally* remove them. Americans should be active players in the realm of domestic and world affairs. And as citizens, we must take serious interest in the decision-making of those we place in office.

However, did we Americans commit capital crimes, as Ayyad suggests? And do he and the 19 terrorists involved in the September 11 attacks have the right to execute us at their own discretion? Is it a capital offense to support the Afghan *mujahideen* ("warriors of God") during and after their conflict with the Soviets and the subsequent Soviet withdrawal in 1989, even if so doing proved to have been a mistake? Does the hatred of the Arab Middle Eastern nations for Israel make it a crime to support the safety and security of Israel? Is it criminal to befriend Arab and Islamic countries like Saudi Arabia, Egypt, and Jordan to develop trade agreements or request use of their land for bases to fight injustice against weaker nations like Kuwait? Is it criminal to attempt to stop atrocities and starvation in Somalia? Did American diplomatic successes and mistakes, actual and perceived, justify the actions of Islamist terrorists culminating in the attacks on September 11? Is the desire to have material things and to pursue happiness for all members of a society punishable by death simply because a segment of America misuses them for immoral personal pleasures? Is it criminal to be a Christian, a Hindu, a Buddhist, or a Muslim who disagrees with another Muslim's interpretation of the Qur'an? In order to avoid a sentence of death, must we all accept the rigid interpretations and standards that these terrorists (or other terrorists) promote?

In their arrogance and misrepresentation of God and all that is good in the world, terrorists unequivocally respond to each of these questions, "Yes!" Americans and the vast majority of the world unapologetically and rightly respond, "No!" Rather, it is the terrorists' murder of innocent people and their commitment to barbarous attacks against those who disagree with them that demands enduring justice.

A Grave New World

Just beneath the surface of America's pursuit of Aldous Huxley's "Brave New World" of technological advances and the inevitable material wealth that accompanies it lurks another world, a dark and dangerous world that takes the very technology that is meant for good and uses it in the gravest of ways. Tainted hearts and twisted minds call upon gods of their own making to inspire them to misuse advances in chemistry, engineering, microtechnology, biology, and genetic engineering to create weapons of terror and mass destruction. The known misuses and potential misuses of technology—the turning of good ideas into evil ones—have awakened civilized humanity to the perils of this Grave New World. Though the motives are complex, the facts are clear.

At 8:45 on Tuesday morning, September 11, 2001, an unprecedented attack against America began. But it wasn't the first time that radical Islamist terrorists had attacked the nation. However, those earlier attacks were in faraway places, making the threat seem distant and oddly tolerable—cruiseships in the Mediterranean, hijacked airplanes on tarmacs in Israel and Greece, military targets on deployment in Beirut and the Persian Gulf, and U.S. embassies on foreign soil. Those acts of aggression and war against America were discussed by the news networks and on talk shows, and many were connected to Osama bin Laden and his al-Qaeda network, but there seemed to be little or no national outrage over the loss of American lives, and very little discussion of retaliation. Some of the discussions in academia and the media even queried what Americans might have done to unsettle our enemies. Rather than blame the murderers, these inquirers dissected their history, political objectives, and psychological turmoil, and were moved by their difficult living conditions, and some even went so far as to blame the victims.

Although terrorist attacks have diminished in their frequency over the years, they have grown more lethal.[7] It took two local and highly lethal acts of terror (the bombing of the Alfred P. Murrah Building in Oklahoma that murdered 168 people and the September 11 attacks in New York, Washington, D.C., and Pennsylvania that took the lives of thousands) to bring Americans together against terrorists and terrorism. Were the more than 10,000 terrorist attacks recorded since 1968 insignificant simply because they killed fewer people and were perpetrated in more remote places? Of course not. They were not insignificant, but now our national attitude and interest in terrorists and their horrible deeds has forever changed.

A World Without Innocents

Today Americans realize as never before that terrorists do not delineate between civilian and military targets. Nor are they content with only a few casualties or hitting targets in faraway places. Between 8:45 A.M. and 10:29 A.M. on September 11, 220 floors of American economic wealth and ingenuity collapsed, the walls of our military structure had been breached, and four state-of-the-art airliners had been hijacked and used as missiles. More important and even more tragic than the loss of these symbols was the loss of several thousand irreplaceable human beings, mostly Americans, who were swiftly and brutally taken from us. And for the thousands of families and friends, life has changed forever. It has changed for the nation, too.

On that surreal morning we witnessed tremendous explosions; we were horror-struck at the sight of people jumping and falling to their deaths to avoid the intense fires; and we were shaken by the catastrophic collapse of magnificent buildings. Thousands were terrified by the ensuing billows of grayish smoke and flying debris that sent people running for their lives, and across the nation we learned that a third plane had flown into the Pentagon. And then there was the news of a fourth plane downed in a Pennsylvania field—forced to do so by the first citizen soldiers of America's newfound resistance to terrorism. In a span of less than two hours, America discovered that each of its citizens—no matter where they live, what they believe, or what they do for a living—is a target of international, religiously motivated terrorism.

Over the next few days we were repeatedly stunned by the full extent of the death and destruction that remained when the dust settled in New York City and at the Pentagon. The war that terrorism had declared against Americans was now in our own backyard, and the nation temporarily put aside ethnic, ideological, political, racial, and cultural differences to come together as one people to support one nation.

The terrorists who participated in and supported the attacks hoped that the destruction of symbols of our financial and military strength and the murder of thousands of noncombatants would divide Americans and break our will to pursue the foreign policy of our choosing. Instead, the attacks created an unshakable resolve to unite the world to strike a lethal blow against terrorists and the nations who harbor them. As President Bush declared in his address to all Americans, "Tonight we are a country awakened to danger and called to defend freedom. Our grief has turned to anger, and anger to resolution. Whether we bring our enemies to justice, or bring justice to our enemies, justice will be done."[8]

"Holy" Hatred Old and New
A Glimpse at the Current Climate

Thirty-five hundred students at a militant religious school *(madrassah)* in Peshawar, Pakistan begin their day's studies with a motivational prayer: "O Allah, defeat the enemies of Muslims and make Islam and the Taliban victorious over the Americans in Afghanistan." And then they begin an inspirational chant, "Holy War! Holy War!" One of books that is used at bin Laden's training camps (called the *Encyclopedia)* is referenced by one of the students in a discussion with western reporters. He says, "Now listen, America, and listen well," and then reads from the manual, "Bomb their embassies and vital centers." He then warns, "That's what I will do to you and your country. I will get your children. I will get their schools, too. I will get all of you." Another student promises that he will kill more people than Mohammed Atta did at the World Trade Center, and still another holding a picture of the Sears Tower in Chicago says, "This one is mine."[9]

The training in these schools is a blend of radical Islamic theology and militant political thought with the end result being a commitment to spreading their perverse corruption of faith through violence—that is, through the destruction and elimination of Allah's enemies.[10] These expressions of unbridled hatred demonstrate beyond doubt the accuracy of President Bush's words on the night of September 11, 2001: "Today, our nation saw evil, the very worst of human nature."[11] From where did this holy bent toward evil come? How did America come to be called "the Great Satan"?

A Combination of Many Turns

Do you remember the first time you tried to open a combination lock? How many turns did you have to make to the right to the first specified number? Then you had to turn the lock to the left, past a specified number and continuing on just one more turn until you reached that number again. Then you had to make one last turn to the right, not all the way around, but just until you came to another specified number. If you turned the mechanism properly and landed on all three specified numbers, it opened—right?

Trying to unlock the motivations or reasons for the intense hatred of so many in the Islamic world toward the West is like trying to get the numbers right to unlock a combination lock—with the added difficulty of the numbers being extremely worn. Not only are the reasons for their hatred many, but they are often based on misrepresentations of reality, associated with a theological expansionism that is required of those who hope to be counted among the faithful, and expressive of a people's humiliation from having gone from being the world's premiere empire in the sixteenth and seventeenth centuries to becoming a part of what is now, unfortunately, called the Third World or the Developing World.

The brutal aggression that originates from this hatred is difficult for Americans to understand. Nonetheless, a few reasons can be identified to help us toward an understanding.

Colonization. In the same way that it can be said that Islam has no monopoly on war, it can also be said that the West has no monopoly on colonization. The expansion theology of Islam had forged a huge empire that covered the Far East (India—the Mughal Empire 1526–1857); Central Asia (the Safavid Empire 1501–1722); and the Middle East, North Africa, Portugal and Spain in Western Europe, and in Eastern Europe as far as Vienna, Austria (the Ottoman Empire 1300–1922). These vast empires began to weaken just after the Ottomans failed in their second attempt to conquer Vienna in 1683. From this time forward, Western forces began to "pick away" at these Islamic empires until the early twentieth century, at which time most of the Muslim world had been brought under the influence of Britain, France, Russia, and the Netherlands. These western forces were not allies, but often antagonists warring with each other to accomplish their own expansionist ends on Islamic soil. The French invaded Egypt in 1798 under Napoleon Bonaparte, while the Russians were taking the Balkans and northern areas of Central Asia (to include northern Iran). The British were also vying for parts of North Africa and southern Iran, and had dominated India.[12]

With these changes, the hope and glory of Islamic expansion had come to an end. Frequently, when people are conquered, they are viewed as second-class citizens or at least feel so. Unfortunately, promises of independence and autonomy are often nothing more than early diplomatic attempts to console the defeated. Generally, defeated populaces resent the fact that they are no longer in control of their destinies. After World War I, Britain and France divided much of the Ottoman Empire (which sided with Germany during the war) and—contrary to their promises of independence—set up protectorates in Syria,

Lebanon, Palestine, Iraq, and Transjordan, to the dismay of the inhabitants.[13]

As a result of more than 200 years of British dominance in India and because of the suppression of Islam after a failed 1857 revolt, a group of Muslims established a *madrassah* (religious school) in Deoband, India (1866) that continues to influence some Muslim attitudes to the present day. The school had two basic objectives: 1) to instill traditional Islamic values in Muslim youth, and 2) *to promote an intense hatred* of the British and all foreign non-Islamic influences. The rigid attitudes and beliefs of Deobandi purists have directly influenced the militant thinking of the Taliban.[14] America, being a non-Islamic state and often an ally of forces that colonized the Islamic world, is thus seen by extension as having imperialistic intentions and, therefore, receives the condemnation and hatred of certain factions within Islam that promote Deobandi objectives or are influenced by similar objectives.

The domination or subjugation of "true believers" (Muslims) by infidels (non-Muslims) is particularly offensive to an Islamic worldview. It is just and good for people to be subjected to an empire expanded and ruled by Muslims, but it is inconceivable that non-Muslims rule Muslims. From an Islamic point of view, imperialism is the evil intent of anyone who attempts to place or places a community of Muslims under non-Muslim rule. However, there is nothing inappropriate or imperialistic in conquering the lands of non-Muslims and subjecting them to the benevolence of Allah and his faithful. The modern-day hostility many Muslims harbor for the West and for America "is surely due to a feeling of humiliation—a growing awareness, among the heirs of an old, proud, and long dominant civilization, of having been overtaken, overborne, and overwhelmed by those whom they regarded as inferiors."[15] It is important to note that America, but for a brief period of time in the Philippines, has never ruled over an Islamic population.

U.S. policy toward Israel. Muslim-Jewish and Arab-Israeli conflict is nothing new. Since the construction of the Dome of the Rock in Jerusalem in A.D. 691, Jerusalem has been Islam's third most holy city, after Mecca and Medina in the Kingdom of Saudi Arabia. Jews, of course, can lay a claim on Jerusalem back to the time of King David and the construction of their temple by King Solomon around 960 B.C. Muslims believe that the Dome covers the rock from which the Prophet Muhammad ascended into heaven to receive the first revelations of the Qur'an. Jews, on the other hand, consider this same rock to be the place where Abraham prepared to sacrifice his son, Isaac, in obedience to God. One thing is certain: The struggle for Jerusalem will continue and tension and conflict between Jews and Muslims is inevitable until the Lord returns to settle the issue. But how did the United States get into the fray? The simple answer for much of the Middle Eastern hatred directed at the United States lies in the fact that America has befriended Israel, the most hated foe of most Muslims.

There were three contradictory promises made by the British during World War I that were left to be sorted out in the postwar years. And those issues are still with us in varying degrees. To the Arabs there was the promise of a united Arab kingdom if the Arabs would revolt against the Turks, who were fighting alongside the Germans. To the Jews there was the promise of a permanent Jewish homeland in return for Jewish support of the allies. To the Europeans there was the promise of ongoing spheres of influence for the French and Russians in the region in return for their participation in the war.[16] The unsettled business of World War I continued up through World War II and beyond. From a problem-solving perspective, the creation of the nation of Israel didn't help.

Oddly enough, the United States was *not* instrumental in the establishment of Israel as a nation in 1948. The significant player "in procuring the majority by which the General Assembly of the United Nations voted to establish a Jewish state in Palestine"[17] was the Soviet Union. In fact, the United States maintained a partial arms embargo on Israel. After the United States helped to secure the withdrawal of Israeli, British, and French troops from Egypt in 1956, Egypt, Syria, Iraq, and others turned not to the Americans but to the Soviets for the purchase of arms.[18] In the end, it appears to have been friendly relationships between the Soviet Union and Middle Eastern countries and anti-American rhetoric that eventually encouraged the United States to seek out a reliable ally in the area: Israel. That Israel has benefited economically and militarily from this relationship further intensifies most Muslims' hatred of both Israel and the United States. To be sure, the difficulties in the Middle East have religious roots, but many other factors, such as this, have complicated the picture.

Failure to modernize. While the Middle East endured colonization, the West was marked by industrial modernization. In the realm of modern government and economic growth, the Middle East fell further and further behind.

Attempts at creating governments that would mirror those of the West ended in failure, with some Middle Eastern nations choosing to ignore the whole idea of a constitution and opting instead for a government that depended solely on the Qur'an (a book that has very little legislative content). Other governments established on a secular basis (a separation of mosque and state), such as in Pakistan between 1947 and 1959, wanted to "create a political arena in which Muslims were not defined or limited by their religious identity."[19] But without strong democratic principles in place, these governments too were doomed to failure. It appears that historical models of leadership (monarchical, feudal, tribal) and different standards within the Islamic community of nations have prevented the creation of an effective and lasting Western-style constitution.

Overall, Middle-Eastern attempts at imitating western democracies and dictatorships (like that of the Soviet Union) have been failures, with many ending in tyranny. Secular Turkey has been the only nation to experience a degree of success with democracy.

To give some idea of conditions in the Middle East, some media sources have said that Afghanistan's economy, especially during Taliban rule, was in the Stone Age. There's much truth to that; the economic policies of the Taliban were abysmal. Other Arab and Muslim nations have fared better but still remain far behind the West in raising their people's standard of living. The lack of economic growth coupled with high birth rate results in extreme poverty.[20] The World Bank said that "in 2000 the average annual income in the Muslim countries from Morocco to Bangladesh was only half the world average, and in the nineties the combined gross national products of Jordan, Syria, and Lebanon—that is, three of Israel's Arab neighbors—were considerably smaller than that of Israel's alone."[21]

Tyranny and poverty search for a cause. Some choose to blame themselves and take the appropriate measures to be the determining factor in their own destinies. And some choose to blame others, blaming the United States for their political and economic woes.

> For vast numbers of Middle Easterners, Western-style economic methods brought poverty, Western-style political institutions brought tyranny, even Western-style warfare brought defeat. It is hardly surprising that so many were willing to listen to voices telling them that the old Islamic ways were best and that their only salvation was to throw aside the pagan innovations of the reformers and return to the True Path that God has prescribed for his people.[22]

The "purists" wanted nothing to do with anyone interested in bringing Western influence into their countries.

Secularism. The West is viewed by Muslims as a godless secular world that threatens Islam's traditional values and theological beliefs. The secularism of the West is materialistic, self-centered, corrupt, and socially unjust, and is wholly without any regard for God. To an extent, this criticism is true. And the West has certainly attempted to reduce, if not eliminate, the influence of religion, especially the Judeo-Christian influence, in society. Many secular advances have rightly made many Muslims skeptical of a style of government (secular democracy) that considers the presence of God in society secondary to the rights and pleasures of the individual.

Though Christian theology is not averse to the separation of church and state in principle (Matthew 22:21; Romans 13:1; 1 Peter 2:13), the idea is thoroughly repugnant and unacceptable to most Muslims, who believe that all of political life should be subordinate to Islamic law and doctrine. While Christians hope to influence culture, they do not in practice believe that religion should be politically forced on individuals, as it had been done so often in the church's infancy (and which in A.D. 312, under Emperor Constantine, became the practice for centuries to follow). As Augustine appropriately admonished, "Faith cannot and should not be forced on anybody." To the extent that secularism has gone well beyond its intended purpose in America, Muslims do have a legitimate concern over the negative influences that secularism can impose on their traditions. But it is unfortunate that they do not understand the influence Christianity had on the very foundation of America's form of democracy. Democracy does not have to be secular; in fact, the more secular it becomes, the more tyrannical it will become.

The secularism of the West is as great a concern to Christians as it is for Muslims. It is unfortunate that Muslims have chosen to view modern Christianity only through the eyes of Christianity's past mistakes and reduce Christians from an honored position as "people of the Book" to the status of an infidel or unbeliever.[23] Such a view has caused many Muslims to hate much of what is truly good about the West and good for the entire world, including Muslims. And the result of this hatred has been manifested in acts of terror by religious radicals.

Though there is much that we disagree over, our common view regarding the dignity of all human life—Muslim, Jewish, Christian, or otherwise—can bring us together to discourage and eliminate views that promote the murder of human beings to achieve or expand one's theological objectives. In the end, the tragedy of September 11 will remind us to stay vigilant about the realities of violence, and that is good. It certainly did nothing to convince the secular world that radical Islamic expansionism is the pathway to a better life.

Faith & Fear

Ours is a world of different philosophies, cultures, religions, ethnic backgrounds, social strata, and personal experiences; yet, we are all the same. Each person who walks on the earth is a created being, made in the image of the one true God. In truth, we are simply one race of human beings, each "fearfully and wonderfully made"—even the terrorists among us. The unity of the church is a major theme in the New Testament, and it reflects the unity of the human race that God envisioned at the creation of Adam and Eve. What were Adam and Eve thinking when they rebelled against God? They misused their gift of freedom to choose a way that seemed right to them (Proverbs 14:12), and disunity and death has followed the human race ever since. Still, God stayed in hot pursuit of His human creation—first through the nation of Israel, and then through the church after the Lord's death and resurrection. His desire for a unified humanity remains the same: "There is neither Jew nor Greek, there is neither slave nor free man, there is neither male nor female; for you are all one in Christ Jesus" (Galatians 3:28).

If we can learn to see each other as God sees us (worth dying for and therefore of limitless value), then we will look at people—Christian or otherwise—through the cross of Jesus Christ. The terrorist wrongly looks through the crosshairs of a weapon; Christians must look through the cross. When we do, we will see others through the eyes of our biblical faith, not through a fear of their doctrines and differences. In so doing we will avoid the blunders and brutality that too often character- ized Christianity from the time of Constantine through the 1600s. The church has no state power to force expansion, and it does not need such power.

Our message belongs to the Spirit and providence of God—we are its delivery system and it is our responsibility to reflect it accurately, lovingly, and wisely. We have accepted God's love for us and, therefore, our eternity is secure; there is no need to fear judgment (1 John 4:17-18). But keep in mind that in a broken world, things get broken. Bad things happen to good people because the world is marred by sin. So beware of danger, and be aware of God's truth. Though we who are Americans love our country and long for its survival, remember that the salvation of the world does not depend upon the continued existence of America. It depends on the providential plan of God. Stay faithful to God, be knowledge- able of his Word, and confident in the Hope that is to come.

Terrorism

What Is It?

Terrorism never loses its essential nature, which is the abuse of the innocent in the service of political power.[1]

Christopher C. Harmon

Terrorism—the word even sounds ominous and foreboding. It is also bewildering. Nearly everyone has some ideas about it, and the images of its results are indelibly etched in our individual and national memories. On the surface, it is as difficult to define as it is to forget. Like the term *cyberspace,* it is a word that is in daily usage around the globe and in the headlines. Yet there is much about it that is confusing. It is a term that is often overused, applied, and misapplied to any abhorrent act of violence in society whether committed by a psychotic individual, a religious fanatic, or a political dissident—or groups of them. We read about terrorist states and state-sponsored terrorists. There are organizations, individuals, networks, and alliances around the globe participating in and supporting terrorism, and there seem to be as many names of individuals and groups as there are causes for which they act.

It is not uncommon to read or hear terms such as economic terrorism, psychological terrorism, environmental terrorism, and a host of other combinations that may have a lot, a little, or nothing to do with the world of politics or international relations. Yet because the term *terrorism* is emotionally charged, it is used in a pejorative manner and often tied to anything the user opposes personally, politically, or philosophically. When used in this way, the term becomes so common and so broad that it loses its true meaning and significance. Like the term *holocaust,* if we apply it to every murder or act of genocide, it is eroded in both meaning and memory.

Changing Times, Changing Meanings

One of the difficulties of defining terrorism is the fact that the term has changed in its meaning and usage since it was first coined. The word comes to us originally from the Latin *terrere,* "to cause to tremble." Though terrorism as a political and religious act has been around for centuries, the *term* as we know it was first popularized in the 1790s during the French Revolution. In the aftermath of the uprisings of 1789 there were anarchy, turbulence, and transition in French national and political life as the nature and face of France's government changed radically. In 1789, thousands of French subjects reduced the reign of the Bourbon king Louis XVI to that of a constitutional monarch. In 1792 the government was again changed as the king was deposed and a republic was declared. In 1793–94, the government attempted to restore order by establishing a system of government known as the *régime de la terreur* and it is from this phrase that we get the English word *terror.* Interestingly, the term was first used in reference to the actions of a government, albeit a recently established revolutionary state.

Although we usually think of the term *terrorism* as referring to an act taken against a government, it was originally used of an act taken by a government against elements within the nation. In the history just cited, the revolutionary French government was acting against counterrevolutionaries, dissidents, and others deemed to be "enemies of the people." Arrest, swift trial, and death by the guillotine of those convicted of treason was the result of the regime of terror. From its inception on September 5, 1793, until it ended in the summer of 1794, more than 500,000 of France's 25 million citizens were jailed as political suspects and enemies. Thousands died in prison, and more than 25,000 were executed with or without trial.[2] Though, like many revolutions, the French Revolution ultimately devoured its own leaders, the Reign of Terror it induced was violent and memorable.

It is also ironic that the word as it was first used was very closely associated with the ideas of virtue and democracy—a usage that is 180 degrees opposite of the contemporary usage. Yet the terrorism of the French Revolution shared at least two characteristics with its present-day progeny. First, it was neither random nor indiscriminate, as it is so often erroneously portrayed today, but rather, it was organized, deliberate, and systematic. Second, like terrorists proclaim today, the goal of the acts of violence and the justification for them was the creation of a new and better political order.[3]

With the coming of the industrial age and the rise of capitalism, new reactionary ideologies also arose, most notably communism and Marxism, and a new era of terrorism began. This era began in Russia and soon spread to Europe, culminating in the First World War and collapse of the Russian monarchy. During this age nationalist movements in Turkey, the Balkans, and present-day Armenia also experienced terrorist acts, giving the term *nationalist* a revolutionary connotation.

By the 1930s and the eve of World War II, the term *terrorism* had changed again and it came to be used to describe the acts of dictatorial leaders against their own citizens. In the shadow of Fascist Italy, Stalinist Russia, and Nazi Germany, the faces of the terrorists were seen as being those of Mussolini, Stalin, and Hitler.

In the years after World War II, *terrorism* once again took on revolutionary connotations and it is this sense that is still with us when we see, hear, or use the term. In these years it was often used in reference to nationalist or anticolonial groups around the world, and several present-day nations partly owe their independence to movements that employed terrorist tactics.

In the revolutionary and tumultuous decades of the 1960s and '70s, terrorism's semantic domain was enlarged to encompass nationalist or ethnic separatist groups working outside of the colonial framework, as well as radical individuals and organizations that were motivated by radical ideologies on many topics.[4]

During the 1980s, terrorism was seen primarily as an action that was state-sponsored by regimes in Iran, Libya, and Syria that were opposed to the United States. During this decade, terrorism was associated with the struggles of smaller states against larger ones, whereby the smaller states could act against the larger without the risk of retribution.[5]

With the collapse of the former Soviet Union and the end of the Cold War, terrorism came to be understood as a part of what analysts called the "gray area phenomenon." This phrase was used to describe threats against the stability of nation states by many different organizations, individuals, and processes. These were nonstate actors using violence against established states in order to create shifts in power or new states. These new actors included segments as diverse as criminals and religiously motivated individuals and groups. The meaning of terrorism was understood to describe a phenomenon with several elements that was part of the growing world of nonstate conflict.[6]

It should not surprise us that the meaning of *terrorism* has shifted through the years, but as it did, a common and agreed-upon definition has become more elusive. What's more, the willingness of individuals to accept the label of *terrorist* has also shifted through the years. Terrorists today often call themselves by names that evoke images of self-defense, military organizations, religious warriors, freedom, and liberation. While some terrorists acknowledge the horrendous nature of their actions, most of them do not see or portray themselves as others perceive them.

Interestingly, everyone agrees that the words *terrorist* and *terrorism* are now pejorative terms to be eschewed and avoided.[7] Equally important is the reason behind this avoidance. Terrorist expert Brian Jenkins writes, "Use of the term implies a moral judgment; and if one party can successfully attach the label *terrorist* to its opponent, then it has indirectly persuaded others to adopt its moral viewpoint."[8] While the slogan "One man's terrorist is another man's freedom fighter" is commonly part of terrorist rhetoric, it is, as we will see, also inaccurate and deceptive.

Definitions: Objective Standards in a Subjective World

Without a definition of terrorism and a basic understanding of it, the fight against it is futile. Ultimately, there can be no genuine prohibition without definition. Ideally, there should be an internationally accepted definition by nations based upon international law so that terrorism can be easily identified and eradicated. While such an agreement is not likely, terrorism *is* definable, and the accepted definitions *are* more similar than dissimilar.

So what do the experts say it is? Since the rise of modern terrorism over the last 30 years, there have been more than 100 definitions of terrorism offered by experts and organizations studying the phenomenon. This is not a new field of study, and the literature on the topic is vast. All definitions agree that terrorism involves violence or the threat of violence, yet it is important to remember that while terrorism is violence, not every form of violence is terrorism.[9] Among the most widely used definitions are these:

Terrorism is...

- ...an act or threat of violence against noncombatants with the objective of exacting revenge, intimidating, or otherwise influencing an audience.[10]

- ...the deliberate creation or exploitation of fear through violence in the pursuit of political change.[11]

- ...premeditated, politically motivated violence perpetrated against noncombatant targets by subnational or clandestine agents, usually intended to influence an audience.[12]

- ...the unlawful use of force or violence against persons or property to intimidate or coerce a Government, the civilian population, or any segment thereof, in furtherance of political or social objectives.[13]

- ...the deliberate and systematic murder, maiming, and menacing of the innocent to inspire fear for political ends.[14]

- ...the unlawful use of—or threatened use of—force or violence against individuals or property to coerce or intimidate governments or societies, often to achieve political, religious, or ideological objectives.[15]

Any of the above definitions are usable, but in this volume, it is the last two upon which we will focus. The first of these is clear and concise: *Terrorism is the deliberate and systematic murder, maiming, and menacing of the innocent to inspire fear for political ends.* This definition was first used and adopted by The Jonathan Institute in Jerusalem at a 1979 conference. The second definition is longer and more specific: *Terrorism is the unlawful use of—or threatened use of—force or violence against individuals or property to coerce or intimidate governments or societies, often to achieve political, religious, or ideological objectives.* This definition, used by the Department of Defense, is significant because it recognizes religious motivations as a primary reason for some terrorist acts. Religion can be a catalyst for peace, but it can also be a trigger for violence and war.

Many Motives, Many Means

People use terrorism for many reasons in an attempt to project or gain power, and their acts are calculated to produce fear. Terrorism is not a spontaneous or random act, but one that is planned, specific, and intentional. It may appear random at first, but it isn't. It is a violent physical and psychological act conducted for an impact on a specific audience in pursuit of political, religious, or ideological goals. The intent is to induce fear in someone other than the victims in order to make a government or audience change its policies or activities.

There are many motives that inspire terrorists to act, but they fall into three broad categories: rational motives, psychological motives, and cultural motives (including religious). While these categories are helpful in understanding the actions of terrorists and in analyzing their profiles, it is also important to remember that no one acts out of a single motive. Motives, whether good or bad, are always mixed. Since motives are mixed, a terrorist will be shaped by a combination of motives. It may be possible (and often is possible) to determine the dominant motive, but a whole profile needs to be created in order to fully understand and combat the terrorist threat.

Rational Motivation—"No Pain, No Gain"

The terrorist who is shaped primarily by rational motivation is a person who evaluates the use of terrorism as a tool much like a military commander evaluates a given military situation for determining a course of action, or like a business entrepreneur analyzes the risks and benefits of entering a new market or attempting a corporate takeover or merger. For the terrorist acting primarily from rational motivation, terrorism is only one weapon available for use in the struggle for power. As despicable as the act is, there is a calculated analysis performed by the rationally motivated terrorist. It is wrong, but it is thought out.

Psychological Motivation—"Hatred of the Heart"

Terrorists who act primarily from psychological motivation do so because of a personal dissatisfaction with life or accomplishments in life. Often these people do not view their own thoughts and actions as wrong or unacceptable. Because they have a polarized mentality of "us versus them," they often project their own actions and motivations onto others. In essence, they demonize their opponents and attribute only evil motives to anyone outside their group. As a result, in their minds, they are able to dehumanize their opponents and victims.

Often, the psychologically motivated terrorist also has a deep personal need to belong to and be accepted by a group. This need can become more significant than any political motive or goal of the group. These individuals or groups will often commit terrorist acts in order to maintain self-esteem and legitimacy, even if the acts are counterproductive to their stated goals.

Cultural Motivation—"Faith, Family, and the Flag"

Cultural values can be among the strongest catalysts there are for engaging in terrorist acts. Those things within a culture by which we identify ourselves or are identified by others can bring the most comfort in times of crisis, but potentially, also the most conflict.

The terrorist who acts from cultural motivation will also often have an "us versus them" perspective or attitude that may be based on ethnicity, religion, or nationalism. When backed into the corner physically, politically, or psychologically, people gravitate toward those things in their lives that bring the most comfort and loyalty, and frequently this is their faith, their family, and their regional or national identity. The most volatile of these cultural motivations may well be religion, because religious beliefs are so deeply held and transcend physical concerns and political values. A threat to a person's religion puts the present at risk as well as that individual's or group's cultural past and future. It is for this reason that terrorism in the name of religion, violence in the name of God, can be especially destructive. Religiously motivated terrorists, like all terrorists, view their acts as morally just and divinely approved or commanded. What would otherwise be an extraordinary act of desperation becomes a religious duty or mission in the mind of the religiously motivated terrorist. This helps to explain why religiously motivated extremist groups and terrorist organizations exhibit a high level of commitment and willingness to risk death or commit suicide in their terrorist acts.

As we will see, religiously motivated terrorism is an extremely complex phenomenon that is not easily overcome. Because the terrorist is acting on the assumption of a divine mandate or religious necessity, many methods of dissuading the violent act are futile. This also means that there must be clear thinking and a correct understanding of the religiously motivated terrorist's perspective.

One Face with Many Masks

Much of this book addresses the issue of religiously motivated terrorism. However, before we look specifically at terrorism initiated for religious reasons, it is vital to remember that terrorism has many masks. Terrorism is not necessarily something that always lurks in the shadows and dark alleys of society and culture. While it is often formulated in less-than-desirable places, it is at times also nurtured behind closed doors in the halls of state power and places of worship. It has been supported by clerics and diplomats, as well as by criminals, dictators, and drug dealers.

State-sponsored terrorism is war by proxy, and among the nations that have sponsored terrorism in recent years are Cuba, Libya, North Korea, Iran, Iraq, Sudan, and Syria. While state-sponsored terrorism is in decline, there is also the practice of using individuals or groups who act on their own or for their own reasons yet have links to particular nations. This is often the case with religiously motivated terrorists. Because they are driven by religious motivations, they are often willing warriors and state surrogates. A rogue nation can use these terrorists as an inexpensive means of creating international chaos. By funding or harboring them, such nations can allow someone else to do their dirty work.

In recent years, especially since the collapse of the Soviet Union, there has been the union of terrorism with organized crime. While organized crime has existed for centuries and terrorists have routinely profited from criminal activities to fund their activities, the line between terrorism and organized crime has become increasingly blurred.[16]

In the 1970s the word *narcoterrorism* entered the vocabulary of the media and terrorist studies. The blending of drugs and terrorism continues in the twenty-first century. Terrorism expert Walter Laqueur writes:

> Originally, the terrorists and the guerillas were mortal enemies of the drug producers and traders. On an ideological level, the revolutionaries opposed the use of drugs and punished those in their ranks who violated this rule. But, over time, the production and smuggling of drugs has been practiced by guerilla and terrorist groups of the left as well as the right, and by others who are neither left nor right but nationalist-separatist in inspiration.[17]

In narcoterrorism, ideology and economics quickly blur and blend together producing an outcome that is volatile, violent, and very well funded. On occasion, religion has also played into this equation. Laqueur notes:

> The Sunni Taliban in Afghanistan and the extreme Shi'ite groups in Lebanon have long maintained that although the consumption of opium and similar drugs is forbidden by their religion, the production and trade of drugs is not. Those smoking opium are severely punished, but the growers of opium are encouraged. Thus Afghanistan under Taliban rule has become one of the main centers of opium production.[18]

In the 1990s, after the fall of the Soviet Union, organized crime began to fill some of the void left by the former government. In the aftermath of the collapse and chaos, crime emerged as a powerful force, especially in places such as Chechnya, the Caucasus, and Central Asia. Drugs, weapons, and nuclear materials are some of the major items smuggled and sold by organized crime, and the collaboration with terrorists merges two enormous and dangerous international networks. Organized crime brings money to the table, and international terrorism brings motivation. The result is global terrorism.[19]

The Bottom Line

Regardless of the definition that a person chooses, or how terrorism is manifested, everyone agrees that terrorism is ultimately about using fear and intimidation for power. Experts may differ on wording or nuances in the definitions, but the bottom line is the same—power. The psychologies, ideologies, and theologies surrounding terrorists and their activities may differ, but the goal doesn't change. Terrorism expert Christopher C. Harmon writes: "Terrorism is about power. The famous remark attributed to Vladimir Lenin, that 'the purpose of terror is to terrorize,' is less direct than it sounds; terror is not an end in itself, but a means to political power....Terrorism has always had one nature."[20]

When the smoke clears, the dust settles, and the sirens have faded into the background, terrorist acts should always be clearly seen for what they are—violent and immoral struggles for power. Whether the targets are the skyscrapers of New York City or the subways of Tokyo, the bottom line is the same. Harmon observes:

> Terrorism is always political, even when it also evinces other motives, such as the religious, the economic, or the social.
>
> But while all terrorism has a political purpose, it certainly is distinguishable—technically and morally— from civil dissidence, other forms of civil violence, or revolution, which are also political phenomena....Terrorism is also sometimes used in conjunction with legitimate forms of political struggle. But alliance with legitimate methods cannot justify illegitimate ones; terrorism remains distinguishable from legitimate methods of political struggle.[21]

Whether cloaked in platitudes or prefaced by prayers, terrorism is always political. Terrorism has one purpose—power, and one nature—violent.

Faith & Fear

The extent to which terrorism succeeds is directly proportional to the amount of fear it creates. In the struggle to solve the problem of terrorism, the fear is the greatest element to understand and overcome. The "fear factor," as it has been called in the popular press and media, is central in the personal and corporate consciousness of citizens and the country. And there is a biblical response—faith. Faith is the antidote to fear. Not faith that is naïve or uninformed, but faith that is grounded in the person and work of Jesus Christ and reflected throughout the pages of the Bible.

Scripture tells us that if we focus on Jesus Christ our Savior rather than on our circumstances, we will have joy and contentment that cannot be taken from us. This is what the apostle Paul wrote to Christians at Philippi while he was under house arrest and facing a trial with a potential death penalty if convicted. He understood very well his world and his circumstances, but he also understood the grace of God, which is sufficient in any and every circumstance. We too must understand our world and circumstances, but we need not fear it, for the same grace that comforted and strengthened Paul is available to each of us as well.

3

Terrorism's Trail of Tears

A Brief History of Religiously Motivated Terrorism

If we achieve martyrdom, this is victory.[1]

Taliban leader

I have no regrets, I acted alone and on orders from God."[2] Those were the words of Yigal Amir, the Jewish extremist who assassinated Israeli prime minister Yitzhak Rabin in November 1995. Earlier in March of the same year, Japanese followers of Shoko Asahara in the Aum Shinrikyo sect released nerve gas in the Tokyo subway system, hoping to hasten the new millennium and an apocalyptic age. Since then we have seen other examples of religiously motivated terrorism, including the catastrophic events of September 11, 2001.

Terrorism that is specifically tied to religion is on the rise. Nearly one-fourth of all terrorist groups worldwide are motivated predominantly by religious concerns, and more than half of the 64,000 recorded terrorist incidents between 1970 and

1995 involved religious terrorism.[3] The percentage since 1995 is considerably higher. Also, no one religion has a monopoly on terror. Much of the present-day interest in and focus on religiously motivated terrorism pertains to radical Islamic terrorism, and rightly so. However, the history of terrorism clearly shows that many religions have had and still have followers who are more than willing to spill their own blood and the blood of others through terrorist acts.

Probably everyone reading this book has some experience or understanding of the power of religion to prompt change in individuals and society. For most of us, these changes have been positive—associated with conversion, redemption, and transformation of personal lives and culture. Our images of religion have also been, for the most part, nonviolent.

By contrast, there are present-day religious activists across the spectrum of religious faiths who are willing to kill and be killed for their views. These people go beyond martyrdom— they become terrorists for God.

Fervent Faith, Deadly Faith

It was the early Christian theologian and apologist Tertullian who asked the question, "What has Athens to do with Jerusalem?"[4] When he penned that question around A.D. 200, he was referring to the relationship between philosophical methods of inquiry and the teaching authority of the Bible. However, the question has been adapted through the centuries to become one that asks about the relationship between the sacred and the secular—i.e., religion and the state, or church and state. In other words, what does religion have to do with politics or with the social order? How people answer this question reveals their worldview and affects their actions in public and in private. A secularist will answer, in effect, "nothing"—religion and government are to be completely separate and isolated. Some religiously devout people will answer "everything"—religion and government are to be spheres of influence that overlap completely. In short, the government should be a theocracy. But there is disagreement on what type of theocracy—Jewish, Muslim, Christian, or something else. Most people in the United States will answer Tertullian's question by saying "something"—there is to be some interplay between religion and government. How much interplay or interaction there should be is part of our democratic dialogue and process. There is disagreement, but there is also dialogue.

Through the centuries, religion has often been a catalyst for war as well as for peace. Religious wars and wars justified by religion—sometimes valid, and sometimes invalid—have left a trail of blood through history. One often-overlooked aspect of religion, warfare, and violence is that of religiously motivated terrorism. Terrorism has a long and violent association with some expressions of religion. Because religion generates such strong emotions, beliefs, and loyalties, it can easily be used to justify violence when its adherents believe there is a divine mandate or it is the will of God to carry out certain actions. Religion can also be manipulated by people advocating secular causes.[5] This is seen in the words of Abraham (Yair) Stern, founder of Lehi, known as the "Stern Gang," a secular Jewish terrorist group operating during the fight for Israeli independence after World War II. Stern used the religious symbols, rituals, and memories of Judaism to call others to violence:

> Like my father who carried his bag
> With a prayer shawl to the synagogue on the Sabbath
> So I will carry my holy rifles in my bag
> To the prayer service of iron with a regenerated quorum
> Like my mother who lit candles on the festival eve
> So I will light a torch for those revered in praise
> Like my father who taught me to read in Torah
> I will teach my pupils; stand to arms, kneel and shoot
> Because there is a religion of redemption—a religion
>   of the war of liberation
> Whoever accepts it—be blessed; whoever denies it—
>   be cursed.[6]

To be sure, not all terrorists are religiously motivated, nor do all religions advocate terrorism. There have been, however, strong connections between some expressions of various faiths and terrorism. In fact, some of the words in our everyday conversations and vocabulary originated in religiously motivated terrorism.

Zealots, Assassins, and Thugs

No religion, including Christianity, has been immune to extreme (and in the case of Christianity, unbiblical) violence by those who pervert its teachings. Three words we often use today are related to religious terrorism. The words *zealot, assassin,* and *thug* are each derived from fanaticism in Judaism, Islam, and Hinduism, respectively.

Zealots

One of the earliest religious terrorist movements was that of the Sicarii, during the time of Jesus, who were part of the Zealots of first-century Judea. The Zealots were a Jewish political party that had religious underpinnings and whose members did not hesitate to use violence, force, and deception in achieving their desired political goal of throwing off Roman rule. Simon, one of Jesus' 12 disciples, was a Zealot (Luke 6:15; Acts 1:13). Interestingly, the Roman centurion who arrested the apostle Paul in the Temple mistakenly believed him to be part of the Sicarii (Acts 21:38). Even after the fall of Jerusalem in A.D. 70, and of Masada in A.D. 73, the Zealots continued their campaign of terror. The historian Josephus tells us that they fled to Egypt and continued their terrorist activities until they were suppressed.[7]

The Sicarii were ruthless in their political struggle and revolt against Rome and moderate Jewish factions. Their name was derived from the Latin word *sica,* meaning "curved dagger."[8] According to Josephus, they used short daggers concealed in their clothing to murder their victims, usually at religious festivals. These terrorists operated particularly in Jerusalem and were extremely effective in terrorizing Jews who cooperated with the Romans.[9]

The destruction by the Sicarii Zealots was broadbased and very effective. In addition to murdering individuals and groups in daylight, they destroyed the house of Ananias, the high priest, as well as Herodian palaces. They also burned public archives in an attempt to destroy the bonds of moneylenders and prevent the recovery of debts, an endeavor that they hoped would paralyze the economy. They also practiced primitive chemical warfare by poisoning wells and granaries used by the Romans and their sympathizers, and by sabotaging Jerusalem's water supply.[10]

The Sicarii were motivated by strong religious beliefs that led them to embrace martyrdom and the fervent hope that, after the fall of Jerusalem in A.D. 70, God would reveal himself to the Jews and physically deliver them from the bondage of Rome. They hoped that just as they had been delivered from slavery in Egypt, so too would they be delivered from the tyranny and oppression of Rome. The Sicarii believed their bloody acts would be a catalyst for their emancipation.

Assassins

A much more prominent and well-known group of religious terrorists are the Assassins. These Muslim terrorists operated throughout the Middle East for more than two centuries, from the eleventh to thirteenth centuries. The Assassins, who were an offshoot of the Ismaili branch of Islam (itself an offshoot of Shi'a or Shi'ite Islam), also mixed messianic hopes with terrorist acts during their years of activity from 1090 to 1275. They originated in Persia, but they soon spread to Syria and other locations in the Middle East. During their time of terror they killed Muslim and Christian rulers throughout the Holy Land, including Conrad of Montferrat, the Crusader King of Jerusalem. In their desire to purify Islam, they struck at the religious and political world of their day and seriously threatened the governments of several states, especially the Turkish Seljuk Empire in Persia and Syria.[11]

The word *assassin* literally means "hashish eater"; the Assassins were known for their ritualistic use of hashish before committing their acts of terrorism. They operated in complete secrecy, and they often disguised themselves as Christians and preyed on Crusaders and Muslims whom they viewed as a threat to their own beliefs and existence. Their primary targets were Muslims of the Sunni branch of Islam. They did not normally attack other Shi'ites or native Christians or Jews.[12] The Assassins viewed their killings, always performed with a dagger, as first and foremost sacramental acts of religion.[13] The assassin's dagger was presented to him by his leader in an act of consecration when he was given his terrorist assignment.

These assassins called themselves *fidayeen,* meaning "consecrated ones" or "dedicated ones." Interestingly, they interpreted the Qu'ran's prohibition against using the sword against other Muslims to mean that the true believer could use other weapons, just not a sword.

The gruesome religious ritual of murder was usually carried out in public places of worship or at gatherings on holy days when there would be many witnesses. The Assassins knew that doing their deeds in open venues meant they were unlikely to escape and thus heightened the possibility of capture and martyrdom for their cause. They were prepared to die for their faith and their actions, believing that if they did so, they were free from the guilt of all sins and gained immediate entry into paradise.[14] This belief is held by many Muslim terrorists today and is a significant point of motivation for religious terrorism.[15]

While the Assassins were the most well-known of the Muslims who were hoping to speed up the arrival of a millennial age through their actions, there were earlier groups who also practiced ritual terror and used specific weapons that would likely preclude escape and invite martyrdom.

Within Shi'ite Islam there is a tradition of millenarian movements in which there is the belief that eventually a *Mahdi* (Messiah or Rightly Guided One) will emerge to lead the faithful in a holy war (*jihad*) to cleanse Islam. While in Christian and Jewish messianic and apocalyptic schemes there may or may not be violence, in Mahdist theology, *jihad* in the sense of an armed revolution is mandatory. This is violence and a holy war that will be directed at the majority of Muslims for the purpose of purifying and cleansing Islam. In order to avoid detection by others and prepare for this time of violence, there is in Shi'ite theology the concept and practice of deception or pious dissimulation known as *taqiyya*. In carrying out this practice, the faithful are encouraged and required to conceal the full extent of their beliefs. Just as armies and warriors practice deception in combat, so also in this spiritual struggle of the sword is there to be deception.[16]

The influence and imagery of the Assassins reached far beyond their small numbers. Though they originated in Persia, the legends about them and their leader, Hasan-i Sabbah, known as "the Old Man from the Mountain," deeply impressed contemporaries throughout the Middle East and in Europe and lasted for generations. Though they failed as a movement in their own day, their legacy was secure. Dr. Bernard Lewis writes that "the undercurrent of messianic hope and revolutionary violence which had impelled them flowed on, and their ideals and methods found many imitators. For these, the great changes of our time have provided new causes for anger, new dreams of fulfillment, and new tools of attack."[17] Regrettably, 700 years later, the methods have changed, but the mindset has not.

Thugs

One of the most unusual but effective groups of religious terrorists came out of India and Hinduism. The word *thug* comes to us from the name of Indian murderers and robbers who systematically strangled travelers with a silk tie as sacrificial offerings to Kali, the Hindu goddess of terror and destruction.

In the theology of the Thugs, Kali, a goddess with many dimensions and names, represented the energy of the universe and, therefore, she controlled life and death. It was their belief that they were required to provide victims to Kali in order to help the goddess keep the world in equilibrium.[18] One Thug wrote of the appeasement of Kali, "Bhowanee is happy and most so in proportion to the blood that is shed....Blood is her food....She thirsts for blood!"[19] (It is interesting that in this scenario humans were killed for a goddess, whereas the Bible clearly teaches that Jesus Christ, who is God, died for humans.) The Thugs believed it was their responsibility to stay alive as long as possible in order to keep killing. Each Thug averaged three murders a year, but some killed many more people. One Thug claimed to have strangled 931 persons.[20]

Thugs believed that death actually benefited their victims, who would enter paradise, and they also believed that they too would enter paradise if they were killed as a result of their actions. Because their actions were motivated by religion, they felt no remorse or regret. One Thug was asked by his British interrogator if there was sorrow for his actions and he responded: "Certainly not....Remorse *sahib?* Never! Joy and elation often."[21]

Active from the seventh century until their suppression by the British in the mid-nineteenth century, the Thugs are estimated to have murdered between 500,000 and a million people. This is a staggering number of victims, especially since each one was killed individually. Hoffman notes, "the Thugs' modern-day terrorist counterparts have rarely been able to achieve anywhere close to the annual average of Thug murders despite more efficacious and increasingly lethal weaponry."[22] That was a very true statement—until September 11, 2001.

Terrorism Around the World
Bloody Belfast—Green, Orange, and Red

A little closer to home for most people in the West is the centuries-old conflict in Northern Ireland. It is a bloody dispute in which people claiming to be Christian on both sides of the controversy continue to engage in terrorism and kill each other in the name of God and nationalism. The so-called "troubles" of Northern Ireland have a long and violent history. The religious wars in Europe's history ended more than 300 years ago—except in Northern Ireland, where the killing continues into a new century and a new millennium. In this beautiful part of Ireland, Catholics from the Irish Republican Army (IRA) and Sinn Fein (the Catholic political party aligned with the IRA) and Protestants from the Ulster Volunteer Force, Ulster Freedom Fighters, and Ulster Defense Association routinely engage in terrorist activities. There are periods of calm and renunciation of terrorism, but the hatreds run deep and the memories are long-lived.

Perhaps more than in any other conflict in recent memory, religion has been used and abused to motivate the participants to conflict and terrorism. On one side of the line are Irish nationalists, predominantly Roman Catholic, who wish to absorb the six counties of Northern Ireland into the Republic of Ireland. On the other side are Protestants who want to maintain loyalty to the United Kingdom. They have lived in Northern Ireland for generations, but are unwavering in their allegiance to the British Union.

Northern Ireland's bloodshed is a result of political, cultural, economical, and historical factors, but the blood is kept flowing by religious hatred and religious identity. The conflict dates back almost a thousand years to the 1100s, when English kings began attempts to bring Ireland under their control. When Henry VIII severed religious ties with Rome in the 1500s, a visible and vigorous religious dimension was added as English Protestants tried to conquer Irish Roman Catholics. In

1609, King James I (sponsor of the King James Bible) confiscated land in the northern Ulster region and gave it to Scottish and English commanders who had defeated the Irish, thus creating a Protestant settlement. Uprisings and conflict continued through the centuries that followed, with blood being spilled on both sides.

In the aftermath of World War I and another Catholic uprising, England granted independence to Ireland, but the Protestants in the six northern counties voted to remain part of Great Britain and established the separate state of Northern Ireland in 1921. In the 1950s, terrorism began as the clandestine IRA acted to force the political unification of Ireland.[23] The swell of violence resulted in large riots in 1968 and 1969, and continues up through today. The British Army has permanent detachments in the streets of Northern Ireland, and terrorists have exported their violence to England.

The heart of the conflict in Northern Ireland is not religious, but much of its history is religious, and there are two distinct religious histories and cultures that continue to perpetuate the conflict. Leaders on both sides of the violence acknowledge that religion is not the sole source of the difficulties, but it is a definite part of the equation.[24] Religion can motivate people to acts of virtue or violence, to reconciliation or revenge. In Northern Ireland, it has more often than not led to violence and revenge. An ancient feud with fresh wounds is kept alive by religion and terrorism. In "Easter 1916," Irish poet and playwright W. B. Yeats wrote of the "terrible beauty" that haunts the people of Ireland and the soul "wherever green is worn." In "Remorse for Intemperate Speech," he captured well the bloodshed, grief, and cries of those who perpetuate the terror and death:

> Out of Ireland have we come,
> Great hatred, little room,
> Maimed us at the start.
> I carry from my mother's womb
> A fanatic heart.[25]

Aum Shinrikyo—Tokyo Terror

Religiously motivated terrorism knows no religious boundaries. This fact is perhaps most clearly seen in the actions of the Japanese religious cult Aum Shinrikyo ("Supreme Truth"). On the morning of March 20, 1995, members of this cult released—in a Tokyo subway station—a fatal nerve gas called Sarin, a chemical weapon that was developed in Nazi Germany during World War II but never used for fear of retaliation. In the aftermath of the attack, Japanese officials found a poem titled "Song of Sarin" in the cult facilities:

> It came from Nazi Germany, a little dangerous chemical weapon, Sarin, Sarin!
> If you inhale the mysterious vapor, you will fall with bloody vomit from your mouth,
> Sarin, sarin, sarin, the chemical weapon!
> Song of Sarin the Brave...[26]

Before that fatal day in the Tokyo subway station, Sarin had been used only twice in history. The first time was by Saddam Hussein and the Iraqi Army against the Kurds in Iraq, and the second time was by Aum Shinrikyo in June 1994 in the city of Matsumoto, Japan.[27]

The Tokyo attack killed 12 people and injured 5,500 and sent shock waves throughout Japan. "Although Japan was hit by a major earthquake in January of the same year and more than 5,000 people were killed, the impact of the nerve gas attack was much larger than that of the earthquake. It was the end of the myth that Japan was a safe country. More shocking was the news that it was done by a new religious group named Aum Shinrikyo."[28] However, the cult's experimentation with biological weapons began before it developed Sarin and included experimentation near U.S. military bases in Japan.[29] Who were these terrorists, and why did they do it?

Founded in 1987 by Shoko Asahara, at the time of the attack the group had more than 10,000 members in Japan and 20,000 in Russia. Still in existence today, the beliefs of the group are a blend of several strands of Buddhism, psychology, yoga, philosophy, Hinduism, New Age mysticism, and Christian elements of an apocalyptic or cataclysmic end of human history and the world as we know it. In short, Asahara took ingredients from many religions and blended them into a recipe for global disaster.

The cult's teachings and the personality of its leader attracted many scientists and intellectuals as well as financial resources, which enabled Asahara to establish ties with disgruntled scientists and military elements in the former Soviet Union. The cult was well-funded and widespread. Believing that Armageddon would occur by the year 2000 and building upon claims of direct divine communication and enlightenment, Asahara acted to expedite the end of the world. Asahara claimed he was a living god who held supreme truth and whose actions could not be questioned.[30]

According to Asahara's twisted theology and perverse psychology, he was the only person who could bring salvation to people outside his cult, but he had to kill them before he could have compassion on them. He justified murder as an act of salvation. He had to destroy the world to save it.[31]

Oregon, 1984—"Guess What's Coming to Dinner"

A little closer to home for Americans was the 1984 biological attack by members of the cult led by Bhagwan Shree Rajneesh in Dalles, Oregon, where 751 people were poisoned by salmonella planted by followers in local restaurants. The motive in this incident, apparently, was not to kill, but rather to frighten off local residents in the small town so that the sect could establish their headquarters in the town without local political, religious, and social resistance.[32] Their attempt failed to bring about the political results they wanted, but the actions became a milestone in religiously motivated terrorism, perhaps foreshadowing what can be done by those who are determined.

Kashmir—Terror at the Top of the World

The partitioning of India and Pakistan in 1947 did many things for two nations that are now nuclear powers, but establishing peace was not one of them. Religious and political differences between Hindus and Muslims in the regions are deep, and hundreds of thousands of people have died in the last half century due to conflict. One geographic flashpoint is Kashmir, which was made part of India even though it has a Muslim rather than Hindu majority.

Border wars and skirmishes have arisen several times over the decades and continue into the present, and Kashmir has witnessed two of the three India-Pakistan wars. Now that both India and Pakistan have nuclear weapons, the potential for a nuclear nightmare at the top of the world is very real. High in the Himalayas, skirmishes continue along what some observers now call "the world's most dangerous border."[33] At elevations of nearly 20,000 feet, rival forces have been entrenched for almost 20 years, and the United Nations has been involved in the area since 1949.

While nuclear war is a possibility in this region, terrorism, much of it religious, is a longtime reality, as evidenced by the hijacking of an Indian Airlines aircraft by Muslim terrorists in December 1999. In a region where there are Muslims, Hindus, Sikhs, and Buddhists, and that has the longest-running conflict in the history of the United Nations, terrorism has become commonplace. There are several groups pursuing rival claims in the region, and since 1989, insurgency and terrorism has increased. Among the groups are the pro-Pakistani Hizbul Mujahideen, the Lashkar-e-Taiba ("The Army of the Pure"), and the independence groups Jamm and Kashmir Liberation Front. Terrorist groups in Kashmir are on the list of official organizations the United States and others are watching with terrorist concerns in mind, and the troubles in Kashmir will not go away soon.[34]

Khalistan—The Sword of the Sikhs

The winds of nationalism blow strong among many groups around the globe. The desire for self-rule, whether among Palestinians, Kurds, or religious people such as the Sikhs in the Indian state of Punjab, frequently results in violence. In Punjab, radical Sikhs of the Khalistan Commando Force routinely practice terrorism to keep their movement alive and call the world's attention to their dream of an independent nation.[35] The Sikhs have a long history of conflict and being persecuted because of their religion. The Sikhs comprise a monotheistic religion that blends elements of Islam and Hinduism and had their origins in the late 1400s and early 1500s.

Early in Sikh history, Sikhs developed a warrior profile as a safeguard against persecution. They have a very militant strand woven into their theology and community life based on a concept known as *miri-piri*. In this teaching, it is understood that Sikhs are to follow both secular and sacred swords of leadership. Because of Muslim attempts to conquer them and Hindu attempts to absorb them, the Sikhs have had to fight to maintain their distinctive culture and faith. But there has also been the desire for a sovereign state, and in this volatile mixture of nationalism and religion, there has arisen violence that continues to grow and spread.[36]

Dreams and Nightmares in the Middle East

Conflict in the Middle East is neither new nor likely to subside anytime soon. What is new is the exporting of that conflict, through terrorism, beyond regional borders to places like Kenya, Tanzania, New York City, and Washington, D.C. And while not all terrorism in the Middle East is religiously motivated (or more specifically, Islamist), much of it is wrapped in the words of Islamic history, theology, and life. There have been Jewish terrorists in the Middle East, and not all of the conflict is exclusively religious. However, much of it is

grounded in the history and theology of Jerusalem's three religions—Christianity, Judaism, and Islam.

No religion is monolithic. That is, no religion has all of its
followers throughout history, or at any given moment, believing
exactly the same thing, interpreting holy writings in the same
way, or applying that religion's tenets in their daily lives uni-
formly. This is certainly true of Islam, which has a diverse and
multifaceted global history. Islam's history is rich and vibrant,
but also violent.

Not all Arabs are Muslims, nor are all Muslims terrorists.
(In fact, about 85 percent of Islam's 1.2 billion followers are
non-Arab.)[37] Most Muslims are not terrorists, and not all the
terrorism done by Muslims is done for religious reasons, but
much of it is and can be seen in the names of groups such as
Hamas ("zeal"), Hezbollah ("Party of God"), and Islamic Jihad.
Other groups with radical Islamist foundations include the
Palestine Islamic Jihad, al-Jihad (a.k.a. Egyptian Islamic Jihad),
and Osama bin Laden's al-Qaeda network.[38] With all of these
groups, loose alliances, shared resources, and common enemies create an enormous network of terror that reaches around
the globe. The slogan "the enemy of my enemy is my friend" is
certainly true when it comes to various terrorist groups. With a
common enemy of the West, strange relationships have
occurred.

One of the most well-known organizations supporting terrorism in the Middle East is the Palestine Liberation Organization (PLO), founded in 1964. The PLO is a secular rather than
religious group, and in the 1970s and 1980s, Arab terrorists
working for the PLO made it clear that they were waging war
for an Arab or Palestinian cause rather than that of Islam. In
fact, some of the prominent leaders within the PLO claimed a
Christian rather than Muslim heritage. While the PLO shares
some of the same goals as religious terrorist groups and has an
equally violent history, its foundations are not religious.[39]

The roots of present-day Muslim rage in the Middle East run deep, and the fruit of that rage has often been bitter and resulted in terrorism. Like the conflict in Northern Ireland, the bloodshed of the Middle East is multidimensional and deep-seated. It is about the past, the present, and the future, and varying interpretations of each. It is about politics, economics, history, nationalism, culture, ethnicity, and religion. And, frequently, it is the flag of religion that is flying when the blood is spilled. The rise of terrorist attacks in the Middle East began in the 1970s and has continued in intensity and breadth to the present. These attacks have done much to ensure that this region remains in the news.

Three of the most visible and radical Middle Eastern groups that have strong religious dimensions and histories in their terrorist activities are those mentioned above—Hezbollah, Hamas, and Islamic Jihad. To be sure, there have been and are other groups, but these are the ones that usually capture the headlines.

Hezbollah. The Iranian Revolution in 1979, led by the Ayatollah Khomeini, did much to energize Islamist militants throughout the Middle East. This revolution is repeatedly held up as an example of the potential for political Islam and extremist views in the present day. One of the first places this militancy emerged was in Lebanon, which was involved in civil war and is a battleground for many national and international factions, including the invasion of Israeli forces in southern Lebanon in 1982. Hezbollah's roots go back a decade earlier to splits within the Lebanese Shi'ite movement.[40]

Hezbollah (a.k.a. Islamic Jihad) is, by its own definition, "an Islamic struggle movement" whose "emergence is based on an ideological, social, political and economic mixture in a special Lebanese, Arab, and Islamic context."[41] This radical Shi'ite group was formed in Lebanon but has strong ties to Iran through the Shi'ite religious school in Qom. Hezbollah is adamant in its belief that there is no legitimacy for the existence of the state of Israel, and it continues its bloody campaign to destroy Israel, priding itself on its suicide attacks. Its goal in Lebanon is the creation of an Iranian-style Islamic republic and the removal of all non-Islamic influences, especially Israel, from the region. Hezbollah is known to have been involved in numerous anti-U.S. attacks, including the October 1983 suicide truck bombing of the U.S. Embassy and Marine barracks in Beruit. It receives significant aid from Iran and Syria. Part of the history and legacy of Shi'ite theology and violence is the perception and reality of oppression. As a minority group in Islam, the members share a strong sense of victimhood and injustice, which then leads Shi'ites to justify their violence.[42] And much of that violence is directed at the United States, which is seen to be the source of secularism, Western values, and many of the difficulties in the Middle East. One Hezbollah document proclaims, "Our way is one of radical combat against depravity and America is the original root of depravity."[43] The perception of religious and political oppression easily translates into a mindset of martyrdom and suicide bombing. And neither Hezbollah nor Hamas have any shortage of willing warriors.[44]

Hamas. While Hezbollah comes out of the Shi'ite branch of Islam, 90 percent of Muslims are not Shi'ite, but Sunni. The most well-known terrorist organization representing Sunni Islam is Hamas. One of the early Islamist (politicized Islam) movements in the Middle East during the twentieth century was that of the Muslim Brotherhood, founded in Egypt in 1929 under the leadership of Hasan al-Banna. While in recent years the Muslim Brotherhood has renounced violence, one of its by-products, Hamas, has not.

Hamas was formed in 1987, and throughout its history it has used both political and violent means, including terrorism, to achieve its goal, which is an Islamic Palestinian state in the place of Israel. Its bloody suicide terrorist campaign has killed hundreds of people over the last few years and shows no signs of slowing down. Members of Hamas have been very active and visible in suicide bombings throughout Israel. While the exact size of the organization is not known, there are tens of thousands of sympathizers with a large fundraising network that reaches even into the United States.

Palestine Islamic Jihad. This group began among militant Palestinians in the Gaza Strip during the 1970s and, like Hamas, is also committed to the creation of an Islamic Palestinian state and the destruction of Israel through holy war. Not surprisingly, the United States has been identified as a major enemy of the PIJ because of its strong support for Israel, but the group has not specifically conducted attacks against U.S. interests in the past. In July 2000, however, it publicly threatened to attack U.S. interests if the U.S. embassy in Tel Aviv is moved to Jerusalem. Like many militant Islamists, the PIJ also opposes moderate Arab governments that it believes have been tainted by Western secularism. The PIJ conducted at least three attacks against Israeli interests in late 2000, and it too has conducted suicide bombings in the West Bank, Gaza Strip, and Israel.

Headquartered in Syria, this group works primarily in Israel and the occupied territories and other parts of the Middle East, including Jordan and Lebanon. Like Hezbollah, it has received financial assistance from Iran and also limited logistic assistance from Syria. This is a good example of state support for nonstate terrorist groups.

Al-Qaeda. Literally at the top of the list of religious terrorist groups being hunted and watched in the war on terrorism is Osama bin Laden's al-Qaeda terrorist network. While a more in-depth look at the history, theology, and ideology of this organization will be given in chapters four and six, some introductory background information is included here.

Al-Qaeda merged several years ago with the group Islamic Jihad from Egypt. Islamic Jihad was responsible for the 1981 assassination of Egyptian president Anwar Sadat. Part of this group and plot was a young Egyptian surgeon, Ayman al-Zawahiri, who has since emerged as one of bin Laden's lieutenants.

One of the religious roots of the Sunni al-Qaeda network is the Muslim Brotherhood, which is the father and grandfather of other radical movements. A second root is that of Wahhabism, an eighteenth-century puritanical Muslim reform movement that came out of Saudi Arabia. A third root is that of Deobandi Islam, a puritanical movement that came out of India in the late 1800s in response to British control of the country. (Deobandi thought later spread to Pakistan, and from there it became the primary religious influence on the Taliban in Afghanistan.)

Formed in the Middle East, al-Qaeda now stretches across five continents in a massive web of men, money, mayhem, and murder. Al-Qaeda was established about 1990 to bring together Arabs who fought against the Soviet Union in Afghanistan. Early on, its recruits were sent to Hezbollah training camps in Lebanon in an unusual Sunni-Shi'ite cooperation against a greater enemy, the non-Islamic West.[45]

In 1998 bin Laden and al-Qaeda issued a document entitled "The World Islamic Front for Jihad Against the Jews and Crusaders," which proclaimed that it was the duty of Muslims around the world to kill U.S. citizens, military members, and their allies. In a decade of death, al-Qaeda conducted bombings in the U.S. embassies in Nairobi, Kenya and Dar es Salaam, Tanzania, attacked the U.S.S. Cole, and claims to have shot down U.S. helicopters and killed U.S. military members in Somalia. There have been numerous plans that were foiled and halted but, tragically, the plot carried out on September 11 was not one of them.

Suicide attacks by militant Islamist groups have not been limited solely to Israel, the Gaza Strip, and the West Bank. Before the attacks of September 11, there had been, in the last few years, suicide bombings in Afghanistan, Algeria, Chechnya,

Croatia, Kashmir, Kenya, Kuwait, Lebanon, Pakistan, Panama, Tajikistan, Tanzania, and Yemen. And there have been other plans, such as the plot to kill Pope John Paul II in the Philippines in 1995.[46]

And the List Goes On

Around the globe, from the Islamist radicals Abu Sayyaf ("Bearer of the Sword") to the Jewish groups Kach ("Thus") and Kahane Chai, which were inspired by New York native Rabbi Meir Kahane and attempted to explode the Dome of the Rock on the Temple Mount, terror in the name of religion continues.[47] Hindu Tamils and Buddhist Sinhalese in Sri Lanka have participated in religious terror in Sri Lanka, and paramilitary militia white supremacist groups holding aberrant Christian doctrines in the United States have also shared in the spilling of innocent blood. Indeed, the history of holy terror is long and gruesome, and it has reached around the world and shed the blood of innocent people for political power in the name of religion. Clearly, spiritual values have consequences, and misguided ones create not only martyrs, but murderers.

Faith & Fear

In the first century, the apostle Paul wrote to Christians in Rome, the capital of the empire, encouraging them to maintain biblical values and standards in spite of the corruption and decadence that they saw daily. He also reminded them in his opening statements of the dangers of exchanging truth for a lie. The immediate issue in Romans 1 was moral actions and values relating to sexuality and to ignore God's standards is to invite disaster. The results of sin are always disastrous, for anytime a person rejects the truths of the Bible, he or she inevitably succumbs to the lies of Satan.

Dedication, zeal, and fervent actions are not reliable indicators of truth. It doesn't matter if you are a Christian, Buddhist, Hindu, Sikh, Muslim, or a member of any other sect or religion. Only God's Word, the Bible, provides true and sufficient safeguards against the false teachings and philosophies of any age—including our own. Either we will be fortified by biblical ideas and standards, or we will fall prey to unbiblical ideas. The many religious expressions of terrorism, regardless of the religion from which they spring, are clear and bloody reminders that there is indeed a spiritual war raging in the universe. But it is between the God of the Bible and the created being Satan, and the victory will be God's.

Throughout history, religiously motivated terrorists of many faiths have acted and continue to act on the basis of aberrant theologies and unbiblical principles. Christians are called to a devotion to God that is focused, fervent, and faithful, but our devotion must also be biblical. Christians serve a risen and returning Savior, the Lord Jesus Christ. In our thoughts and actions we must serve Him "who gave Himself for us to redeem us from every lawless deed, and to purify for Himself a people for His own possession, *zealous* for good deeds" (Titus 2:14, emphasis added).

Terrorism's Theology
Cosmic Conflict in Worldly Warfare

> For the religious terrorist, violence is first and foremost a sacramental act or divine duty exe-cuted in direct response to some theological demand or imperative.[1]
>
> **Brad Hoffman**

No one who has seen firsthand or even secondhand the effects of terrorism can fail to be moved by its violent and destructive nature. The graphic images we see through the media only affect one of our senses—sight. But there are also the sounds and the smells. Trauma, tragedy, and tears are always a part of the effects of terrorism, yet religiously motivated terrorists interpret such things as being good, necessary, and desirable. Evil becomes good, twisted by aberrations of faith and misinterpretations of scriptures. Dreams become nightmares and the stench of death becomes incense in a religious act of violence that is divinely ordained. For the terrorist, there is symbolism, sacrifice, and sacredness in the slaying of the innocent.

For anyone looking at the results of religiously motivated terrorism, the questions that must be asked are these: What is it in religions that normally have such an enormous capacity for healing, hope, and restoration that permits them to be used for such destructive acts as terrorism? What is it in their beliefs that makes terrorists martyrs in their minds and murderers to others? What is the theology of these terrorists? What do they believe?

Mental Mindsets and a Mission from God

When terrorists act from religious motivations, they are, from their perspective, committing horrendous acts for more than just strategic reasons and goals. Their acts become sacred moments, they are literally instances of holy terror. As the Bible indicates, the actions of our hands always flow from the attitudes of our hearts. What we think affects what we do, regardless of whether we perform acts of charity and compassion or trauma and terror. Violence is a destructive display of power, and terrorism is a specialized form of violence. It is a tool used to destroy political entities by shedding innocent blood.

In the movie *The Blues Brothers*, actors John Belushi and Dan Ackroyd played the parts of Jake and Elwood Blues, two musicians who, after moments of religious calling, raised money to try to save the Roman Catholic orphanage in which they spent their childhood. Their actions caused chaos and broke many laws, but they always justified them by saying, "We're on a mission from God."

Similarly, but far more seriously, religiously motivated terrorists are acting on the belief that their activities are sanctioned and commanded by God (or other perceived deities). There is a mindset of a spiritual struggle that is overlaid on or worked out through the belief system of the terrorist. Thus, whether one is talking about terrorists who are Muslims, Jews, Christians, Hindus, Buddhists, or any other group, there is a common misperception that is filtered through their specific religion. Their terrorist acts are committed not just for some strategic political goal, but as part of a religious mission from God.[2] In their thinking, not only is their mission performed in the name of God, but it actually originates in the mind of God and the will of God and is then passed on to the terrorists as God's special agents on earth. The terrorists believe that they are acting in the name of God.

Heavenly Warfare on Earthly Battlefields

Religion can reduce violence or produce violence, and no major world religion shuns violence in every instance. But warfare and terrorism are not the same, except in the minds of religious terrorists. And in their minds, violence is morally acceptable and divinely sanctioned.

Religious terrorists believe that the world and society are in chaos and disorder and believe that their actions are key moments in which they are initiating sacred order and structure on secular culture and society. After analyzing many specific acts and terrorist attacks by religious terrorists, Mark Juergensmeyer writes: "I found in all of these cases that religious language is combined with specific attempts to impose perceptions of order on disorder."[3] Why is this new order necessary? It's because there is a cosmic spiritual conflict raging in the universe that is spilling over into human history. The sacred and the secular are in conflict because good and evil are struggling. "Those who attempt to impose their notion of order feel that there is a basic conflict between the two, and the battle between order and disorder is ultimately waged on a cosmic plane."[4]

On the battlefield of planet Earth, the terrorist's targets are carefully chosen for their symbolism, real and perceived. Juergensmeyer notes that in almost every recent example of terrorism, "the building, vehicle, structure or locale where the assault has taken place has had a symbolic significance."[5] Things like buildings, planes, power systems, subways, and computer systems represent power. They are cultural, social, and political centers. Thus, an attack on a military installation or force, an assassination of a political leader, or the destruction of a financial system or network, are seen by the terrorist as hitting at the heart of the enemy. Targets are not random choices. "When one attacks such a place, be it an airport or the World Trade Center or the Kasumigaseki subway station in central Tokyo, one challenges the power and legitimacy of society itself."[6]

The violence may not always be symbolic, but it is always real. Juergensmeyer writes, "What about real acts of religious violence? The death squads of Sikh and Sinhalese revolutionaries, the terrorist acts of Lebanese and Egyptian Muslims, and the religious soldiers of Jewish and Christian activists are all engaged in violence in significantly non-symbolic ways."[7] Spiritual justifications in no way diminish the horror of the terrorist acts and there is no legitimate moral, ethical, or theological justification for such acts. They are always wrong. The deaths are real, and the violence cannot be legitimately condoned in the name of God.

Contemporary religious terrorism is usually dated from the rise of the Iranian revolution in 1980 and the religious shock waves and violence that were felt throughout the Middle East in the ensuing years. In the decade following the revolution, the number of religious terrorist groups increased exponentially and spread around the globe. By the late 1990s, almost half of all known, active international terrorist groups were primarily religious in motivation or character. And not coincidentally, the most serious and devastating of the attacks all had religious motivation at their core.[8] However, their basic theological and philosophical perspectives were not new.

Same Song, Different Verse

As we saw in chapter 3, the connection between religion and terrorism is not new, and neither are the religious beliefs and ideas behind terrorism. Belief of a struggle between good and evil is a very old religious and philosophical idea known as *Manichaeism*. The Manichaean black-and-white view of the world dates back to the third century after Christ and was founded by an Iranian philosopher named Mani, who synthesized Persian, Christian, and Buddhist ideas in his teachings. In the West, Manichaeism was fought as a Christian heresy. In Manichaeism there are two worlds—the world of Light and the world of Darkness—and there is a continual struggle between the two. Salvation comes through hidden knowledge to those who seek it through ascetic practices. Much like the Greek philosophy of Platonic dualism and the Christian heresy of gnosticism, in which a god of light and a god of darkness are locked in eternal struggle, Manichaeism separated the world into good and evil, black and white, material and immaterial.

In this dualism, there is an oversimplification of life and creation and of human responses to it. While religious terrorists would deny the heretical roots that are at the foundation of much of their theology, regardless of the religion, they are still there. There are no new heresies in the world—just different manifestations of old ones.

The Terrorist's Trinity

Not only is the number of terrorist acts committed by religious terrorists increasing, but so also is the lethality and body count increasing. For example, from 1982 to 1989, Shi'ite Islamic terrorists were responsible for 8 percent of all the incidents but 30 percent of the fatalities.[9] And the numbers continued to grow throughout the 1990s and into the present decade. Why has this happened? It is because of what terrorism expert Brad Hoffman calls the core characteristics of religious terrorism. He writes:

> The reason why terrorist incidents perpetrated by religious motives result in so many more deaths may be found in the radically different value systems, mechanisms of legitimization and justification, concepts of

morality, and world-view embraced by the religious terrorist compared with his secular counterpart.

For the religious terrorist, violence is first and foremost a sacramental act or divine duty executed in direct response to some theological demand or imperative. Terrorism thus assumes a transcendental dimension, and its perpetrators are consequently unconstrained by the political, moral or practical constraints that may affect other terrorists.[10]

These characteristics which drive religious terrorists can be seen in what can be called the terrorists' trinity or triad. Think of a triangle with its three corners connected by lines. At each point is one portion of the trinity. One corner is sacrifice, the second is martyrdom, and the third is religious warfare. When religious conflict and specifically religious terrorism occurs, these three elements are frequently present. Thus, Juergensmeyer writes:

> It seems to me that the line between the symbolic and the real is frequently a blurry affair, and that the themes of sacrifice, martyrdom and religious warfare intertwine in virtually every tradition. They are conceptually linked. They are all about destruction, of course, but more importantly they are about human destruction on behalf of a divine purpose. For that reason, they are related; each can be explained in terms of the others. Sacrifice can be regarded as a symbolic form of warfare or as a symbolic form of noble self-destruction (martyrdom); martyrdom can be seen as the internalization of sacrifice or of war; and religious warfare can be viewed as a litany of sacrifice and martyrdom.[11]

In religious terrorism, the acts are committed with the intent of helping God or the sacred order triumph over the disorder of the secular or everyday world. Violence is justified as a means to creating a new order and a new world. It may not be the one you want, but it is the one terrorists want, and the one they think God wants.

Common Characteristics

There are several characteristics that typify the actions of those who commit religious violence and religious terrorism.[12] Those traits are:

- *Incarnational*—The terrorists think that a cosmic struggle is being played out in history. When this happens, the terrorists perceive the spiritual struggle between good and evil as one that is carried out in the headlines of the world's newspapers and the hearts of the faithful and the faithless. From their perspective, this is not just history, philosophy, or theology—it is daily life. Spiritual warfare becomes real or physical warfare, and the key warriors are the terrorists themselves.

- *Identity*—The terrorists identify personally with the struggle. Not only is there a raging war of good and evil occurring in time and space, but the terrorists also see their own actions and themselves as integral to the conflict. With a mentality of "an offense to God is an offense to me," they begin to identify personally with the cosmic conflict. They are intimately involved and have no desire or intention to accept or overlook it.

- *Integrity*—The terrorists believe that the cosmic struggle continues in the present. There may be much real and perceived history to the struggle, but it is one that is understood to be raging in the present, whether it is in the headlines or not. In fact, it may be that terrorists sometimes act because it is not in the headlines.

- *Immediacy*—The terrorists think that the struggle is at a point of crisis. From their viewpoint, the scales of

history are about to tip in the direction or either good
or evil. Therefore, now is the time to act. Victory or
defeat in the cosmic struggle is at hand. Therefore the
terrorist act becomes necessary to serve either as a catalyst or capstone for victory.

- *Importance*—The terrorists believe that the acts of
  violence they commit have a cosmic meaning. Because
  the struggle is primarily spiritual in nature, the terrorist
  act is very important. It is so important that it is seen to
  have literally earth-shattering ramifications that will
  receive the applause and approval of heaven.

Bombs, bullets, and blood are all very real, and so are the
people who use them in the name of God. While there are
times when military force is necessary and justified, that is far
different from the violence wrought by terrorism. "There is a
difference between wars justified by religion, however, and religious wars. It is one thing when the moral sanction of religion
is brought to bear on such worldly and non-spiritual matters as
political struggles. It is quite another when the struggles themselves are seen primarily as religious events."[13]

Ten Traits in Terrorist Theology

There are many themes or traits in religiously motivated terrorism, and normally there will be several present that can be
easily identified either in the act itself or in the history or statements of the organization and its members. Traits to look for
include:

1. A belief in and mentality of a multifaceted crisis

2. A belief and perception that the actions of the terrorists are defensive and resisting secularization

3. A belief that the movement of which the terrorist is a
   member is a pure movement or cause

4. A belief that the constituents of the terrorists' movement have been alienated from society

5. The belief that the acts of terrorism will lead to a religious state or millennial age

6. The belief that there is an all-out war in which the terrorists are participating both spiritually and physically

7. The belief that any compromise is impossible since the terrorist acts and causes are divinely ordained

8. The belief that the terrorists have been divinely chosen and that their acts of terror have divine approval

9. The belief that because the conflict is primarily spiritual there must be an all-out struggle to resist secularization

10. The belief that key events in both recent and distant history have made the actions necessary

In effect, religious terrorists completely overlap their cause with the will of God and the plans of God. They perceive themselves to be special agents of God in a spiritual war that has erupted onto the headlines of daily life. Because they believe they are doing God's work, they think they cannot and will not fail.

Walking the Walk and Talking the Talk

Many religious terrorists and their organizations can be readily identified by their propaganda, personalities, names, and actions. Some of the common characteristics here are:

- A name that reflects religious roots or a monopoly on truth—for example, Hezbollah—"Party of God," Hamas—"Zeal," Aum Shinrikyo—"Supreme Truth," "Army of God," and "Soldiers of God"

- The visible emergence and presence of militant clerical and religious leaders
- The use of religious language, ritual, and symbolism in the terrorist acts, writings, and propaganda
- The importance of holy days and anniversaries in conjunction with the terrorist attacks

Careful study of various groups and the analysis of specific terrorist acts shows that there is reason and logic behind those acts. The acts are not random; they are calculated and they have strong religious overtones. They are wrong, but they are religious.

A World of Difference

In the minds of religious terrorists, there is literally a world of difference between the violent acts they commit and the acts committed by secular terrorists.[14] What are some of the differences? For the religious terrorist the basis of an act of terrorism is religious or sacramental, whereas for the secular terrorist the act is purely political. Secular terrorists often shy away from massive indiscriminate violence and large numbers of casualties, viewing such things as counterproductive. Not so with the religious terrorists, who seek the destruction of those perceived to be the enemies of God. For them, large numbers of casualties are considered both morally justified and a necessary expedient. Indeed, the more the better.

Religious terrorists are also acting for no one but themselves and God. They are not seeking to appeal to actual and potential sympathizers, as do secular terrorists. Because of that, there is no need for restraint in their actions. The religious terrorist is not acting for publicity, or news, or money and also will not be swayed by public opinion, bribes, or reason. With no social, cultural, or ethical restraints, the potential for doing the unthinkable—whatever that is—becomes very real. There is a single focus: complete the mission for God, at any cost.

For religious terrorists, potential targets and victims are unlimited, especially if the conflict is seen as a global one in which there is a completely new religious world order to be established. The religious terrorist is much more likely to use pejorative terms when speaking about his enemy than is the secular terrorist. In contrast, the victims and targets of secular terrorists are more likely to be localized and focus on political enemies. This is in part because the aims of the two types of terrorists are different, even though their actions and the resulting losses are equally repugnant. Secular terrorists use terror for utilitarian reasons to achieve a desired political goal, while religious terrorists have religious goals and grand schemes for God as part of the aims of their murderous and destructive acts. In the mind of the religious terrorist who sees himself as acting in God's name, there are no grays in the world. There is only black and white, good and evil. As one terrorist responded when asked why civilians rather than military personnel were killed, "There are no innocents in this war."[15]

Finally, secular and religious terrorists have different self-perceptions and different views of their acts. Religious terrorists consider themselves outsiders to the political system they are attacking, and they believe that the system, whatever it is, is not worth saving. It must be eradicated and replaced with a new and divinely sanctioned system. Thus, Hussein Mussawi, the former leader of Lebanon's Hezbollah, remarked, "We are not fighting so that the enemy recognizes us and offers us something. We are fighting to wipe out the enemy."[16] This new system may be a theocracy replacing a democracy, or some other form of a divine dynasty replacing a dictatorship. Whatever is in place must go—God wills it. This is not the view of the secular terrorist, who is using violence as a way of correcting real or perceived flaws in a political structure. For the secular terrorist, violent acts may (or may not) come as a last resort or with reluctance, while for the religious terrorist, such an act may be the first salvo in a war to establish the rule of God.[17]

Messiahs, Martyrs, and Murderers

Religiously motivated terrorists are willing to murder others and become martyrs in their own eyes because they believe that God has ordained and ordered their actions. Frequently accompanying this perspective is the belief that the world is on the verge of some sort of millennial or messianic age which will be ushered in by the terrorist acts.[18]

Similar to religiously motivated terrorist acts are "holy assassinations," in which the assassin acts on what are perceived to be divine orders. Two such assassinations were those of Egyptian president Anwar el Sadat in 1981 and Israeli prime minister Yitzhak Rabin in 1996. One of Sadat's assassins declared, "What I have done, I have done for the sake of God, the Merciful, the Powerful." And Rabin's assassin declared, "I did what I did for God and the Israeli people."[19] Rabin's assassin further claimed that he had "no regrets" because he "acted on orders from God."[20]

One theme that is frequently seen in religious terrorism is that of martyrdom, and there is a strong history of martyrdom within Islam.[21] Martyrdom is especially strong in Shi'ite Islam. While there is debate within Islam over the validity of terrorism and of suicide terrorists as martyrs, there are clearly many who hold to it, aberration or not. Many Muslim terrorists, wishing not to be seen as approving of suicide in their bombing acts because suicide is forbidden in Islam, refer to such acts as "sacred explosions."[22] One terrorist proclaimed proudly, "We do not have tanks or rockets, but we have something superior— our exploding Islamic human bombs. In place of our nuclear arsenal, we are proud of our arsenal of believers."[23]

Arming for Armageddon—On the Eve of Destruction

Weapons of mass destruction (WMD) are no longer beyond the realm of possibility for contemporary terrorists. Since the collapse of the former Soviet Union, concerns about "loose nukes" and "suitcase bombs" have increased. Fears that scientists previously employed in the weapons and military sectors of the Soviet Union might sell their knowledge to terrorists are very real. And terrorists have also made several attempts over the past few years to purchase materials for nuclear bombs. One such buyer was Osama bin Laden, whose plans were foiled when his money was stolen. He lost the money, but not the desire.

Stolen chemical and biological agents are a reality, and as Jessica Stern, a former National Security Agency staff member who ran the Nuclear Smuggling Interagency group, states, "Because chemical and biological agents are relatively easy to produce, a single person with the right expertise could design an entire weapons program."[24] And the problem of stolen nuclear material is a very real and ongoing concern. As one offical in the Russian Ministry of Atomic Energy stated, "The question is not whether large quantities of highly enriched nuclear material will be stolen, but when."[25]

Would a religiously motivated terrorist use biological, chemical, or nuclear weapons? Yes, as they already have in the case of the Aum Shinrikyo cult in Japan. Their difficulty wasn't their desire, it was their delivery.

The Islamic Impulse—Islam vs. the Infidels

"In the wake of secularism, and after years of waiting in history's wings, religion has made its reappearance as an ideology of public order in a dramatic fashion: violently."[26] Perhaps nowhere is this statement truer than in the rise of militant and radical Islam. Islam is just as diverse as every other religion and is practiced around the world. There is a spectrum of belief and practice within it and part of that spectrum is very violent.

The validity of what radical Islamists practice is the subject of an ongoing internal debate in Islam and beyond the scope of this book, but the ramifications of their actions are in the headlines and reach around the world.[27] In their attempts to completely politicize their faith and in their desire to impose their worldview on others, radical Muslims have created global concern and worldwide terror.

While many political leaders, academics, and practicing Muslims and Christians in the Middle East and the West deny that the battle against international terrorism is a battle against Islam, militant Muslim terrorists do not believe that. Osama bin Laden and others clearly believe that they are in a battle that is fundamentally spiritual. The war against terrorism may not be religious to the United States and coalition forces, but the adversaries believe that it is religious. Osama bin Laden's statements are filled with religious verbiage and calls to holy war against the United States and other perceived enemies of Islam.

On the one hand, Muslim leaders in the United States have declared that "Islam is a religion of peace," and on the other hand, taped messages from bin Laden and public demonstrations supporting him in several countries show clear support for Islamist violence. Why is this so?

The spiritual and intellectual roots of Islamist rage and terrorism run deep. They are found in the history, theology, and the political life of Islam. Terrorists such as bin Laden draw on medieval Islamic sources and interpretations that argue that the killing of innocents or even Muslims is permitted if it serves the cause of *jihad*, especially against the West.[28] So what is *jihad*?

Jihad

Jihad, often translated "holy war," has always been a strong force in Islam, but it also has been one that causes much confusion. Rudolph Peters writes:

> The Arabic word *jihad* (verbal noun of the verb *jahada*) means to strive, to exert oneself, to struggle. The word has a basic connotation of an endeavour towards a praiseworthy aim. In a religious context it may express

a struggle against one's evil inclinations or an exertion for the sake of Islam and the *umma,* e.g. trying to convert unbelievers or working for the moral betterment of Islamic society ("jihad of the tongue" and "jihad of the pen"). In the books on Islamic law, the word means armed struggle against the unbelievers, which is also a common meaning in the Koran. Sometimes the "jihad of the sword" is called "the smaller jihad," in opposition to the peaceful forms named "the greater jihad."[29]

Jihad is both a personal and corporate commitment within Islam to spread the faith. The greater jihad is the personal struggle that a Muslim wages against sin and all that is against Allah. It is a personal battle for righteousness. The lesser jihad is the struggle against the enemies of Islam. It is a holy war waged in the name of Allah and according to the will of Allah.[30]

The concept of jihad goes back to the wars fought by the Prophet Muhammad and the written reflection of them in the Qur'an, in which there is frequent mention of jihad and fighting.[31] One question Muslims ask is this: Are Muslims to fight only defensive wars, or are offensive wars permitted and encouraged? This has been an internal and ongoing debate, but the classical Muslim interpretation of the Qur'an favors offensive war as a duty to preserve and enlarge the *umma,* the unified Islamic people. Peters writes:

> The crux of the doctrine is the existence of one single Islamic state, ruling the entire *umma.* It is the duty of the *umma* to expand the territory of this state in order to bring as many people under its rule as possible. The ultimate aim is to bring the whole earth under the sway of Islam and to extirpate unbelief: *"Fight them until there is no persecution (or: seduction) and the religion is God's (entirely)"* (K. 2:193 and 8:39).[32]

Why is this necessary? Because the world is divided physically and spiritually into two realms known as territories or houses.

The House of Islam and the House of War

Jihad consists of several aspects, but the form that is of greatest concern to non-Muslims of the world involves the expansion of Islam—that is, physical confrontation.[33] As noted earlier, the word *jihad* literally means "striving" or "struggle." It was "usually cited in the Koranic phrase 'striving in the path of God' and was interpreted to mean armed struggle for the defense or advancement of Muslim power."[34]

The divinely mandated defense and expansion of Islamic power through physical confrontation is understood through the division of two realms, which are ideological, political, and theological: *The House of Islam (dar al-Islam),* in which Muslim rule and law prevail, and *The House of War (dar al-harb),* in which resides the rest of the world, the unbelievers or infidels. Between the two houses, "there was to be a perpetual state of war until the entire world either embraced Islam or submitted to the rule of the Muslim state."[35]

This form or expression of jihad and the Muslim desire for a unified Islamic community, coupled with militant Islamic views of Israel and the West, form the foundation for much of the hatred that is seen in modern-day terrorist activities. In a "smaller world"—a technologically linked global world—the gulf between the two realms becomes nonexistent, and conflict inevitable. Will Islam and the West ever coexist peacefully? Not if terrorists have their way. For them the West is still the world of the Crusaders both in rhetoric and reality, and there is a radical incompatibility between Islam and the West, be it secular or Christian.

In addition to the revolution in Iran in 1979, there are several other movements that helped with the rise of contemporary Islamic unrest and terrorism. Two of those movements are Wahhabism, which originated in Saudi Arabia, and Deobandism, which came out of colonial India.

Wahhabism

Wahhabism has a history of more than 250 years. Its founder was Muhammad ibn Abd al-Wahhab (1703–87), a theologian who launched a campaign of renewal and purification of Islam. Closely tied to the political history of Saudi Arabia in the last hundred years, Wahhabism has grown significantly as a major religious force in Islam. Secularization in the region and the lack of economic development has made Wahhabism very attractive to those who are struggling socially, economically, and religiously against the perceived secularization of Islam.

For those who follow Wahhabism and other militant movements, the West is a clear enemy because of its modernizing, secularizing effects on Muslim life. Bernard Lewis writes:

> From their point of view, the primary struggle is not against the Western enemy as such but against the Westernizing enemies at home, who have imported and imposed infidel ways on Muslim peoples. The task of the Muslims is to depose and remove these infidel rulers, sometimes by defeating or expelling their foreign patrons and protectors, and to abrogate and destroy the laws, institutions, and social customs that they have introduced, so as to return to a purely Islamic way of life, in accordance with the principles of Islam and the rules of Holy Law.[36]

This desire to purge the nations begins in the Muslim nations and accounts for much of the internal struggles in those various countries, and then extends to the West.

Deobandism

The second strand of Islam for some terrorists, especially those linked with Osama bin Laden, the al-Qaeda network, and the Taliban, is that of Deobandi Islam. This strand of Islam arose after the bloody "Revolt of 1857" in India. Although this uprising was tied to a grassroots nationalist movement in India, much of the blame was placed on Muslims in India by the British. Muslims within India wishing to separate themselves politically from the British and religiously from Hindu influences began to follow a puritanical Islamic movement founded in a school in the city of Deoband.

The school in Deoband taught an intense hatred of the British and all foreign (i.e., non-Islamic) influences and also possessed a zeal to indoctrinate Muslim youth with Islamic values.[37] Following Indian independence and the creation of Pakistan, many Deobandi schools were started in Pakistan. These schools also drew heavily from Afghanistan and espoused a hatred for the West and all things non-Islamic. It is in part students coming out of this tradition that comprised the Taliban.

The sources of strife in the Middle East are many, and certainly not all the blame is to be placed at the feet of Islam and militant Islamists.[38] However, some of it rests there. Much of the religiously motivated terrorism in today's world has Muslim roots, and the fruit of that tree is not only bitter, it is deadly.

Faith & Fear

Religiously motivated terrorists are right about one thing: there is a spiritual battle going on in the world. But they are dead wrong in their understanding of its character, course, and final outcome. They are also wrong in their interpretation of who is to fight and how they are to fight. We do not win spiritual battles by terrorism, nor does God call Christians to either terrorist acts or religious crusades.

In Ephesians 6:10-20, the apostle Paul reminds Christians that there is indeed spiritual warfare in this world, but that the weapons of that war are also spiritual. The "full armor of God" (6:11) is not comprised of Kalashnikov assault rifles, rocket-propelled grenades, and weapons of mass destruction. Rather, the weapons we are to use are faith, truth, righteousness, salvation, prayer, and the Word of God. In 2 Corinthians 10:3-4, we are told that "though we walk in the flesh, we do not war according to the flesh, for the weapons of our warfare are not of the flesh, but divinely powerful for the destruction of fortresses."

Christians are to be involved and engaged in the world, and we are called not to impose our values, as religious terrorists do, but to attract people to God. It is a fine line we must walk. Authentic biblical faith and a concern for and commitment to justice and righteousness should be one of spiritual cause and effect. Because we have salvation and are growing in faith and being conformed to the likeness of Jesus Christ, we then reflect those realities through our actions and works. And we do so with the Word of God in our hands and the Holy Spirit in our hearts, calling all people to allegiance to Jesus Christ, the Light of the world. "For the crisis of our times, the Light that shines in darkness is still more than adequate."[39]

Terrorism's Tactics, Targets, and Trends

The Danger of Being Different

You have to be lucky all the time—we have to be lucky just once.[1]

Irish Republican Army slogan

Everyone has heard the whimsical statement, "Just because you are paranoid, it doesn't mean they are not out to get you." Contemporary terrorists might use a variation: "Just because you aren't paranoid, it doesn't mean they aren't out to get you." Terrorism is a threat to personal, national, and international security. It will continue to be a problem for democracies as long as individual terrorists have resources to carry on their work and various states to harbor and sponsor them. Brian Jenkins, one of the world's foremost terrorist experts, believes that we have now crossed a new threshold in terrorist activity. Political ideology has been

85

usurped by religious ideology. Muhammad has overtaken Marx.

Jenkins believes that "large-scale, indiscriminate violence is the reality of today's terrorism....as we move into the twenty-first century, we face serious danger."[2] Why does he say this? Because he sees that the trends have changed. He writes:

> The replacement of ideology with religious fanaticism as the driving force behind terrorism eroded the self-imposed constraints that had limited terrorist violence in the past. God's self-appointed avengers killed without concerns about alienating constituents. Large-scale indiscriminate violence had become the reality. The new terrorist adversaries viewed America as their battleground.[3]

Jenkins argues that the fight against terrorism is just and necessary, but will also be protracted and costly. The tactics of terrorists are changing, and so too must ours.

> Having spent 30 years tracking the trajectory of terrorism, I am skeptical of those who promise to end it. That is not a realistic objective. We face a long, often frustrating campaign that will demand unwavering resolve, creativity and cold, calm courage.

> There will be no Normandy landings to console us. No inexorable liberation of enemy-held territory. No terrorists will surrender on the decks of a U.S. battleship. No victory parades. No clear signals....Action against terrorists will provoke further violence. But inaction on our part will not persuade terrorists who have declared war on the United States to suspend their operations. Either way, terrorist attacks will continue....Will Americans stay the course? We have no choice. Protecting everything is not possible. Withdrawal is not an option. The defense of our nation directly depends on our ability to reduce the capability of the terrorists to attack us. This time it is different.[4]

Why is it different? Because for those fighting terrorism there is now a recognition that terrorism has reached a critical stage in our global health. No longer is it an irritation or nuisance that brings minor discomfort. It is a catastrophic and deadly cancer. For the terrorists, this time is different because they now have new tactics, targets, and trends.

What's Next?

Religiously motivated terrorism and terrorism with casualties in the thousands rather than dozens or hundreds has now become the new benchmark. The 9/11 attacks have become the standard against which future attacks will be measured and compared. And for those watching the trends prior to 9/11, the signs were ominous:

> During the final years of the twentieth century, the number of terrorist attacks worldwide declined, but the number of casualties per attack rose. Experts felt the latter trend was ominous. They generally agreed that the risk of a catastrophic attack was still low, but worried that a new kind of terrorist driven by fanaticism and hatred rather than limited political objectives might try to cause true mass destruction. They were right to worry.[5]

After the 9/11 attacks, terrorists will likely choose a different method of attacking their targets. James M. Lindsay, a former National Security Council director, states, "They look for the places where you are vulnerable and attack you there, when they can catch you flat-footed. They are always looking for the places where you're not looking. They study you."[6]

Terrorism is not random indiscriminate violence. It is plotted, calculated, and timed for effect. There are patterns and trends in terrorist activities. An understanding of some of these things will enhance counterterrorist endeavors, though such endeavors will not completely eliminate the potential of terrorist violence.

Tactics from the Arsenal of Fear

Historically, terrorists have used a limited range of activities and methods in their attacks. From the 1970s to 1990s, six tactics comprised the vast majority (as much as 95 percent through 1985) of the attacks. Those tactics were:

- bombings
- assassinations
- armed assaults
- barricade-and-hostage situations
- kidnappings
- hijackings

Of the six methods listed above, bombings accounted for more than half the attacks, and no terrorist group used all of the tactics.[7] Over the years, as security measures were enhanced and as government concessions to terrorists decreased, tactics changed. As a result, the defense against terrorism is difficult. The ability to quickly change tactics increases defensive preparations and costs against such actions.[8] Additionally, terrorists can spend months or years preparing for their attacks and can have several courses of action available to them for each strike. Jenkins observes that "the decline in some tactics and terrorist targeting has been offset by a trend toward attacking softer targets. In this regard, terrorists always have the advantage. They can attack anything, anywhere, at any time. We cannot possibly protect everything all of the time."[9]

While the weapon of choice for most terrorists remains the assault weapon and small bomb or grenade, the events of 9/11 clearly demonstrate increased lethality in some attacks. As far as tactics and weapons are concerned, the 9/11 attacks were low-tech endeavors. The attacks were coordinated, and the planes loaded with fuel became the weapons. What's most significant about the attacks was the willingness of the attackers to die. Brian Jenkins writes:

The terrorists' secret weapon on September 11 was not technology, but human resolve. Coordinated attacks can succeed only if those carrying them out are willing to sacrifice their own lives. That these attackers did so wiped out several assumptions about suicide attacks. Analysts had previously viewed suicide attacks as not easily exportable....

The principal perpetrators of the September 11 attacks, however, had lived in the United States for months beforehand, leading apparently normal lives, interacting with society, in some cases, traveling abroad. They had ample temptation and opportunity to change their minds, but they did not do so.[10]

Mass casualties were not new in the months and years prior to 9/11. But how high can the numbers go? Is there a limit to the number of victims a terrorist or terrorist organization will create? The fear is that the answer is now a resounding *no*. The possibility that terrorists might obtain or develop nuclear, chemical, or biological weapons has given terrorism the potential for the ultimate weapon and the ultimate tactic. Thus, terrorism expert Walter Laqueur observes:

Weapons of mass destruction are a fact of life today. We have seen the nuclear arms race intensify in Asia, and elsewhere the production and use of biological and chemical weapons....It is entirely possible that the terrorist of the future—tomorrow, perhaps—will avail himself or herself of one of these weapons. In addition, the electronic age has now made cyberterrorism possible. A onetime mainstay of science fiction, the doomsday machine, looms as a real danger. The conjunction of technology and terrorism make for an uncertain and frightening future.[11]

Thus, to the six tactics above, two more can now be added:

- Weapons of mass destruction (WMD)
- Technological and information disruption

Force Multipliers—A Bigger Bang

One of the unique things about technology and terrorism is the way that technology impacts terrorism as a force multiplier. From a military perspective, a force multiplier is something that increases the striking power of an individual, unit, or army without increasing the numerical strength of that entity. A force multiplier permits its users to add to their aura and give the impression that there is the capability of fighting at a higher level than resources permit.

Today there are four prominent force multipliers for terrorists—technology, transnational support, media, and religion. What do these four things do? A lot. Technological weapons or making targets of technological sites gives the impression of complex and sophisticated tactics by a terrorist organization. When an organization such as al-Qaeda has transnational support, there is clearly the ability for larger strikes. Global movement and the potential of reaching across borders and continents brings a terrorist organization greater attention and often, greater financial support.

Media coverage also increases the knowledge of terrorist activities by repeatedly running their stories and sensationalizing them. A camera can be a strong tool in the toolbox of terror. And religion is the final multiplier because it has changed the entire structure of contemporary terrorism by removing the moral constraints to which terrorists previously adhered. Each of these multipliers allows a terrorist or terrorist group to function as if they were a larger and more powerful force.[12] Perceptions are critical, especially when they relate to power, and it is power that terrorists crave.

Targets, Not Bystanders

In the submarine world, there is a saying that there are only two kinds of ships—submarines and targets. Likewise, for the terrorist there are only two kinds of people—terrorists and targets.

From their perspective, there are no innocents, no noncombatants, and no exemptions. Clearly such was the case on September 11, 2001. Brian Jenkins writes, "Terrorists may target anything that symbolizes a government, ethnic group, ideology, economic system, policy, or point of view they oppose....It is difficult to find a country without American diplomats, American businessmen, American missionaries, American reporters, or at least American tourists."[13] Jenkins' statement was written long before terrorism came to American shores; what he said in the mid-1980s is even more valid today as a global war against terrorism is underway.

The targets of terrorists are not randomly selected. They are chosen with a great deal of planning, usually over a period of months or even years. The selection is normally a two-phase process. In the first phase, targets are identified on the basis of their political suitability for being a foe of the terrorist or the supporters of the terrorist. Someone or something is deemed "guilty," such as the Pentagon, which symbolizes American military strength, and the World Trade Center, which symbolized American economic strength.

The second phase of the target selection assesses the feasibility and mechanics of the attack. This phase involves in-depth planning, surveillance, rehearsing, and staging prior to the attack.[14] Phase one is the *who* and *what*, phase two is the *how* and *when*. Target selection today includes not just people, planes, ships, and buildings, but also institutions such as the media.[15] In today's world any person who thinks he or she is exempt from a terrorist hit list is gravely mistaken. To be sure, most people will not become victims of terrorism, but some will.

Jessica Stern, a former member of the staff of the National Security Council, writes, "Successful terrorists will choose their technology to exploit the vulnerabilities of a particular society. Modern societies are particularly susceptible to weapons that are capable of killing many people at one time— weapons of mass destruction (WMD)."[16]

Why would they even consider choosing such a weapon? Because, regardless of the weapon, tactics and targets are tied to power and are chosen because they are considered the best means to an end. Bruce Hoffman notes that because terrorism is the deliberate and planned application of violence, there are several processes functioning to achieve the goal of power. "Violence (or the threat of violence) is thus the *sine quo non* of terrorists, who are unswervingly convinced that only through violence can their cause triumph and their long-term political aims be attained."[17] Terrorists will thus commit acts of violence with the hope of sequentially gaining:

- attention

- acknowledgment

- recognition

- authority

- governance[18]

To be sure, most terrorists do not achieve their ultimate goal. Usually only the first three of the above are achieved, but that will not keep them from trying. And the greater the region or population the terrorists want to govern, the greater their attempts. "For them, the future rather than the present defines their reality."[19] The desire for greater power requires the blood of more victims.

Deadly Misconceptions

Since the 1970s, when terrorism began to be seriously studied by authorities and academics looking at the patterns, profiles, and psychology of these acts, there have been several misconceptions identified about terrorism. Consciously and unconsciously, assumptions have been made by those involved in counterterrorism and by the public. When these assumptions are wrong, the price of the mistake is frequently paid in human lives. Christopher C. Harmon states well the concern:

> Despite much experience and data in such fields as criminology, journalism, political science, and psychology, important misconceptions still obscure terrorism. Its nature as an implement of power and politics is often veiled. Some of its characteristics remain unseen. The result is that some public discussions of terrorism are barren, and counterterrorism policy at home and abroad is sometimes misdirected.[20]

What are these misconceptions? Harmon has identified five of the deadliest:[21]

1. *Perception*—Terrorism is at times philosophically defensible.
   Reality—Terrorism is never moral.

Terrorists use several lines of argumentation to ethically justify their actions, but in the end, what they do is obscure the fact that terrorist acts are a fundamental abuse of human rights and terrorism morally affects everyone, whether they are targets or not. In an age when many people have abandoned the possibility of moral absolutes and objective truth, the terrorist mantra "One man's terrorist is another man's freedom fighter" becomes an easy sell. It's pithy, memorable, and implies that the violence is for a noble cause. There may be some superficial similarities between a terrorist and a freedom fighter, but they are two distinct profiles. To accept the above slogan is the equivalent of saying, "One woman's rapist is another woman's romantic."

A second ethical argument put forth is that terrorism is the only means the weak have against the strong. Harmon writes, "Reason dictates that the weak possess many natural rights. But how does this include a right to terrorism? It is an odd argument that begins in moral regard for an aggrieved smaller party but then is used to morally justify abuse of a yet smaller entirely apolitical group."[22] This argument ignores the fact that terrorists, if they consistently followed this line, would permit any aggrieved individual to use violent acts to change the status quo. Every person could be the Unabomber, and the result would be global anarchy. "Instead of some injustice, the world would have no justice at all. Terrorist spokesmen never discuss this simple extension of their own logic, and reporters and social scientists usually fail to insist they discuss it."[23]

The third ethical argument used by terrorists is one of attempting moral equivalence. Terrorists will argue that the violence they commit is no worse than the violence used by states and their agents—law enforcement and the military. While abuses certainly happen in the fight against crime and in times of war, such abuses are not morally sanctioned under just war theory and the rule of law. Accepting the moral equivalence argument denies the validity of the just-war principle of noncombatants and proportionality, which will be discussed later. National and international laws and rules of engagement are created to prevent such abuses. There may be, tragically, occasional violations or abuses of them, but these exceptions should not be allowed to become logical ammunition in the terrorist's arsenal.

The logic of the terrorist is, in the end, faulty and futile. Harmon writes:

> The reality that terrorists and their apologists will not face is that a moralizing argument for immoral activity can be a useful lie, but only for the short term. Ultimately it is only by way of legitimate political principles and activity that any group, revolutionary or ruling, can exercise power morally and reasonably.[24]

Terrorists engage in acts of violence against the state and its citizens to gain power, and if they are successful and themselves become the rulers, they must then continue the abuse of individuals to maintain that power. Today's successful terrorist is tomorrow's ruthless dictator. A terrorist outside the palace gates is a tyrant inside them. "The moral arguments of terrorists and their supporters are thus emptier than spent cartridges."[25]

2. *Perception*—The political left and political right are true enemies.
   Reality—The left and the right are extremes, but not enemies.

The enemy of the left and the right is usually those in the center. The perception that "the left and the right are simply fighting each other so let them go at it" is not historically valid. While in different countries they have fought each other, many times it is the innocent ones in the center who are their victims. Harmon notes:

> Ostensibly enemies, left and right spill more printer's ink than blood over their differences. Nearly all their violent acts are aimed at the democratic, peaceful center which lies between them; it is the government that is most hated by extremes of the left and right.... Both extremes also detest the mass of civilians, even as they seek their support. The public is thought to be inadequate, unenlightened, and almost inhuman—"the walking dead" is a phrase used by terrorists of the 1960s and 1970s and by philosophers favored by such groups.[26]

3. *Perception*—Terrorist acts are random and mindless.
   Reality—Terrorist acts are cold and calculated.

The fact that terrorist acts include the element of surprise makes many people think that they are spontaneous and random. Yet, as noted earlier, the attacks are planned and practiced. The acts are intentional. The destruction can be catastrophic, but the attacks are comprehensible. "Behind the screaming and the blood there lies a controlling purpose, a motive, usually based in politics or something close to it, such as a drive for political and social change inspired by religion....The terrorist is not usually insane; he or she is more usually 'crazy like a fox.'"[27]

4. *Perception*—Terrorists are poor, unemployed, and uneducated.
Reality—Contemporary trends and profiles show just the opposite.

Some terrorists are indeed recruited into movements because of unemployment and a perceived lack of options. Some are also poor and even illiterate, but that is not the norm. The examples of Osama bin Laden, the Unabomber, terrorist pilots, terrorists attempting to acquire and use weapons of mass destruction, and the threat of cyberterrorism all show a demographic shift in the profile of the terrorist.

Part of this shift includes an increased level of religious education for many terrorists. Religiously motivated terrorists are frequently well-versed in a curriculum of political propaganda and twisted theology.[28] The Taliban, named from the Pushtun word for "student," arose from the religious schools educating Afghan refugees in Pakistan. Gaza City's Islamic University has been a very public breeding ground for Hamas. Yigal Amir, who assassinated Israel's prime minister Yitzhak Rabin, was a student, and Baruch Goldstein, who killed 30 Muslims in a Hebron mosque, was a physician.[29] Today's terrorists are grossly misled, but they are not ignorant—and that increases the threat.

5. *Perception*—Terrorists are almost always men.
Reality—There are a large number of women terrorists.

Trends in terrorism over the last couple of decades have shown that there are many female terrorists and movement leaders who are female. "There really is no male 'norm.' By one estimate, more than 30 percent of international terrorists are women, and females are central to the membership rosters and operational roles in nearly all insurgencies."[30]

Women are active in many terrorist organizations throughout Asia, Central America, and South America, and some are among the most wanted. Additionally, they have been active in Europe and in some Muslim organizations, especially in Iran.[31] Convicted Red Brigade (Italian) terrorist Susanna Ronconi bluntly stated, "It is the woman who gives life; it is the woman who also takes life."[32] In an extensive study of women terrorists and after interviews with many of them, Eileen MacDonald writes that those she interviewed echoed one opinion: "Some people can kill and others cannot. It does not matter if you are a man or a woman."[33]

The perceptions and misperceptions about terrorism are important and affect antiterrorism defensive measures and counterterrorism operations. They also affect public and private perspectives on a global problem. How terrorism is viewed and understood will determine how it is fought. And the most important thing is how it is defined at its core. Harmon is correct when he states that "one could argue that if terrorism is not immoral, then nothing is immoral."[34]

A Clash of Civilizations?

What's on and over the horizon with regard to terrorism? That depends on how you view the world. Do you think that globalization and current trends are toward integration or disintegration? And more importantly, what do terrorists think?

Samuel P. Huntington of Harvard University has presented an acclaimed and controversial model for the future of international relations that argues that religion will continue to be a major and growing factor in hearts and headlines around the world. In contrast to those who presume or foresee an international arena of unity, cohesion, progress, and the worldwide embrace of democratic capitalism led by the West and deference to Western values, Huntington offers a totally different perspective. He contends that in the post-Cold War era, and for the first time in history, global politics has become multipolar and multicivilizational. The future is not political optimism, but political pessimism, and not unity, but fragmentation.[35]

The conflict, Huntington believes, is inevitable, and the former rivalry of superpowers is being replaced by the "clash of civilizations." "In this new world, the most pervasive, important, and dangerous conflicts will not be between social classes, rich and poor, or other economically or politically defined groups, but between peoples belonging to different cultural entities."[36] A big part of those cultures is religions.

Huntington's model identifies eight distinctive civilizations:

- Islamic

- Sinic (centered on the core state of China)

- Western (centered on the United States)

- Orthodox (centered on Russia)

- Japanese

- Hindu

- Latin American

- African

Of these eight entities, the conflicts will arise in part due to the arrogance of the Western civilization, the intolerance of the Islamic one, and the assertiveness of the Sinic one. The most dangerous places for conflict are along the "fault lines" between civilizations, and the greatest potential for conflict is between Islam and the West.

Huntington's model is controversial, but to the extent that it is valid, there will be bloodshed, and religion will likely be an enormous catalyst for such conflict.[37] What does that mean for terrorism? It is very significant, and many of the writings about terrorism are applying portions of Huntington's thought.[38] As part of the spectrum of political conflict and war, terrorism may be among the first sparks from this clash and, therefore, there may well be a lot more of it. If so, then current efforts to diminish global terror are not only good, but mandatory.

Trends Today and Threats Tomorrow

What specifically should we be looking for as we read the headlines, watch the news, and live with terrorism as a daily topic of conversation and concern? Regarding the past, the present, and the future of terrorism, Simon Reeve notes:

> The men and women who dominated international terrorism until the 1990s were a murderous bunch. Using plastic and home-made explosives, they blew up buildings, shopping centres, planes and trucks, killing thousands of innocent people and maiming many thousands more. But according to intelligence analysts they could be the terrorists of the past.

> In the years to come, warn the experts, terrorists will not stop at blowing up a building, they will want to threaten an entire city, or even a whole nation, using weapons of mass destruction (WMD). Their arsenals will contain nuclear bombs, and biological and chemical weapons. It is the stuff of nightmares.[39]

If Reeve is correct, then 9/11 may be a gruesome preview of "coming attractions."

Four things are agreed upon by those who watch terrorist trends closely:

- increased lethality

- technological adaptation

- worldwide reach

- religious radicalism

The events of 9/11 show that each of these trends are realities today. Those attacks also show that combinations of the four trends are inevitable. On 9/11, all four were present. The reality of today's terrorism—and tomorrow's—is that of brutal, bold, and bloody violence. And the real questions are how much, when, and where?

Faith & Fear

Terrorism denies the human dignity of individuals by intentionally destroying those who are created in the image of God. It is an abuse of all biblical teaching on the legitimate role of the state, the sanctity of life, and the use of just force. The Bible emphasizes the dignity and worth of every human life. But Scripture also emphasizes that physical survival is not the highest of all values. Eternal life is more important than the present life. That in no way means that we are to deny the value of individuals or disregard their rights, either individually or collectively. There is a legitimate use of force and punishment, but such uses are the function of the state and not of individuals.

Yet the ramifications of the fall in the Garden of Eden have touched all of the created order. No one is immune from sin and sinful actions. When, in Genesis 4, Cain killed his brother Abel, the pattern for conflict among and between people and nations of the world was set. Terrorism, like murder, is an intentional use of violence to take life. It usurps the state, and every act of terror is a sin against others, the state, and God.

Christians are called to proclaim the gospel of Jesus Christ and the truths of the Bible in and to a world that increasingly rejects the possibility of moral absolutes and divine revelation. The clash of civilizations is important in international relations, but more important is the clash between naturalism in all of its forms and the supernaturalism of the Bible. And in the midst of this clash, Christians are called to be foot soldiers of the Savior. Whether we die a victim's death at the hands of terrorists, a martyr's death at the hands of those who deny the gospel of Jesus Christ, or a natural death when taken by the hand of God unto Himself, we are to be faithful witnesses in a fallen world.

Yesterday is history, tomorrow is hope, today and this moment is what we have for certain. We are not called to fatalism but to faithfulness in the midst of and in spite of the terrors of the day. For those who have eternal salvation because of personal faith in the person and work of Jesus Christ on a cross 2,000 years ago, there is no fear of the present or the future. It is the apostle Paul who reminds us in Romans 3:38-39, "I am convinced that neither death, nor life, nor angels, nor principalities, nor things present, nor things to come, nor powers, nor height, nor depth, nor any other created thing, will be able to separate us from the love of God, which is in Christ Jesus our Lord."

Terrorism, the Taliban, and a Tangled Web

A Worldwide Cast of Characters

> We—with God's help—call on every Muslim who believes in God and wishes to be rewarded to comply with God's order to kill the Americans and plunder their money wherever and whenever they find it.[1]
>
> **"Jihad Against Jews and Crusaders"**
> *Written and signed by Osama bin Laden and others*
> *February 23, 1998*

T errorism is both a national and an international problem that touches every continent and most of the world's nations. It is not just an issue of national security; it is an issue of global security. Though much of the recent focus in the United States has been on the al-Qaeda network of Osama bin Laden, that is only part of the problem. Each year the U.S. Department of State publishes a book-length report entitled *Patterns of Global Terrorism*. In the year 2000, in the months before the 9/11 events, there were 423 international terrorist attacks, including the bombing of the U.S.S. Cole.[2] The numbers are increasing each year, and the terrorist organizations are proliferating. Al-Qaeda is one of the most prominent organizations in the news today, but it is far from the only one. Terrorism is found around the world, and terrorists can also reach around the world. Part of the concern of those fighting terrorism today is the fact that it is not only a worldwide phenomenon, but terrorists also have the potential to strike anywhere they want. With technology and globalization, regional conflicts are easily exported around the globe. It's easier today for terrorists to make their presence felt than ever before. Fortunately, there is also an international cooperative effort to eradicate terrorism. Though it will never be 100 percent effective, it can make a significant impact. Fighting terrorism today means more than "not in my backyard." It must mean "not on my planet." As one terrorism expert stated, mocking the often-heard "One man's terrorist is another man's freedom fighter" slogan, "One democracy's terrorist is another democracy's terrorist."[3]

Killing the Hydra

In Greek mythology there is a story about Hercules killing a creature known as the *hydra*. The hydra was a monstrous dragon with nine heads. Each time a head was cut off in battle, it was immediately replaced by two new heads unless the wound was cauterized. Hercules was eventually victorious in his conquest of the monster, but not without great effort and determination. So too will it be for the ongoing fight against terrorism. It will be a multifaceted battle of which military force is only one aspect.

Once you start pulling the string on terrorism networks to identify their sources and resources, it doesn't matter whether they are motivated by religion, nationalism, money, ethnicity, or something else. The networks, both formal and informal, are large, multinational, and often well-funded.

Terrorism is a moving and changing target. Organizations, personalities, causes, sympathizers, resources, and training often overlap and merge. In addition, there is frequently a criminal element mixed in with terrorist activities. Illegal drugs, weapons, and financial transactions are commonplace in terrorist organizations. Terrorists will often use criminal activities to fund their operations. Small things such as credit-card theft and extortion become sources of cash for terrorists. Yet, not all funds are raised through illegal means. A lot of money is raised through legitimate enterprises such as the honey business and, in the case of Osama bin Laden, the sale of tanzanite gems. Some terrorists are set up in businesses that blend into local communities and then funnel their funds back to the parent organization.

Global terrorism involves both formal and informal networks of terrorists. Some have a common vision, and others are very diverse in their goals. We are not saying that there is a worldwide conspiracy of terrorists. Rather, there are some conspiracies that have a worldwide reach and effect. And there are other groups that are willing to share their resources with likeminded individuals and organizations against common enemies. One organization that operates on several levels is al-Qaeda.

Al-Qaeda—Here, There, and Everywhere

In the 1800s there was a saying that "the sun never sets on the British Empire." It was so large that somewhere in the world, the sun was always shining on a territory or colony flying the British flag. Today, that same slogan could just as easily be applied to the terrorist network al-Qaeda, which was formed by Osama bin Laden. What is unique about this network is that as a movment it combines centuries-old theology with contemporary technology in a global mission without borders. "A defining characteristic of the movement's development has been its success in combining two seemingly incompatible sources of strength: a conservative interpretation of Islam and a comfort with aspects of the modern world that have given birth to a highly mobile, popular, wealthy, technologically savvy transnational enterprise."[4] Part of what is unique about al-Qaeda and other contemporary terrorist organizations is the shift away from the state-sponsored terrorism of the 1970s and 1980s. The new terrorists are transnational and borderless.

Al-Qaeda is larger than many multinational corporations and has more money than the national budget of some countries. Its global reach spans more than 50 countries and five continents, and its resources are in the billions of dollars. The organization is thought to have active cells in more than two dozen countries ranging from Canada to Chechnya, Belgium to Bangladesh, and Ethiopia to Ecuador. And yes, even in the United States, in places such as Florida, Texas, Maine, Louisiana, New Jersey, New York, Minnesota, Washington, and California.

The origins of the al-Qaeda terrorist network go back to the war against the Soviet occupation of Afghanistan, which began in 1979. During that time, many Muslims came to Afghanistan to help the local *mujahideen* fight the Soviets. One of those who came was Saudi billionaire Osama bin Laden. Working out of Peshawar, Pakistan, the resistance fighters came under the spiritual influence of a Palestinian leader named Abdallah Azzam, who had established an organization to provide aid to the *mujahideen* and also to give religious training to the warriors. This organization came to be known as al-Qaeda al-Sulbah, "the solid base." It was the embryo that would eventually grow into an international terrorist organization.

Also in Pakistan at this time was Ayman Al-Zawahiri, an Egyptian doctor with a long record of participation in militant Islamic politics. Al-Zawahiri was part of the assassination of Egyptian president Anwar Sadat in 1981, and he led a group known as al-Jihad, which merged with al-Qaeda, in the 1990s.

Azzam was killed in 1989 by an explosion while on his way to prayers, but the organization and momentum were not stopped. The Soviets left Afghanistan in 1989, but the al-Qaeda members did not. They stayed and trained for the future. By this time a conscious decision was made to keep al-Qaeda functioning and growing in order to spread a purer form of Islam around the world through violence. Bin Laden and others in the organization realized that if thousands of warriors could be imported and trained to fight in Afghanistan, then they could be sent elsewhere to continue the fight for radical Islam. From bin Laden's perspective, if the Soviet Union, a world super-power, could be defeated, then so too could others, including the United States. If a *jihad* in Afghanistan was possible, then why not in America and elsewhere? Why not "around the world in eighty jihads"?[5]

Initially the targets of al-Qaeda were the moderate governments of Saudi Arabia and Egypt, but with the onset of the Gulf War and the presence of the U.S. military in Saudi Arabia, the United States became a target as well. With the ongoing struggles and civil war in Afghanistan in the 1990s and the subsequent rise of the Taliban, al-Qaeda had a secure location from which to run its training camps for local and global operations. The training camps were originally set up in Sudan and then, in 1996, in Afghanistan. At more than a dozen camps thousands of terrorists were trained and then sent back to their own countries or elsewhere to spread their plague of terror.

While the original al-Qaeda members were veterans of the Soviet-Afghan war, younger members are aligned with other conflicts, such as those in Chechnya and Bosnia. As in so many terrorist organizations, there is a fluid nature to al-Qaeda so that it is constantly changing and developing, thus making it harder to track and attack. While many of the fighters known as *Afghan Arabs* came from Muslim countries in the Middle East to fight the Soviets and later align with the Taliban, some did not.

Today, al-Qaeda reaches out and appeals to a broad range of potential recruits, drawing from Islamic idealists and intellectuals as well as disgruntled and disposed individuals across the

Islamic world. Al-Qaeda has also recruited U.S. citizens over the last ten years.[6] There are numerous al-Qaeda members who were raised as Muslims in communities throughout Europe. This means that they can easily fit into local areas and travel readily throughout Europe and other locations. They are known as *Takfiris* because they have adopted an extreme Islamic ideology known as *Takfir wal Hijra* ("Anathema and Exile"). They blend in with local society and culture, and they are ruthless. That is a dangerous combination. One French official stated that they seem, on first glance, to be "regular, fun-loving guys—but they'd slit your throat or bomb your building in a second."[7]

After training, some of the Afghan Arabs returned to their own countries, like Algeria, where they formed splinter groups such as the Groupe Islamique Armi (GIA). Founded in 1991, the GIA is one of the most brutal terrorist groups in Africa, contributing to the deaths and disappearances of more than 100,000 Algerians in the last decade. Others moved to Somalia, Kenya, and Sudan.[8]

Working much like a franchise business, al-Qaeda sets up and assists terrorists around the globe who share a common religious vision for the "pure" practice of Islam and the eradication of its enemies. Al-Qaeda will provide instruction, guidance, and seed money for terrorists to set up business in their own country, as well as fund the international movement of terrorists.

As an organization, the al-Qaeda network is structured with bin Laden as the founder and leader, and a ruling council, or *shura*, functions much like a corporate board of directors. These lieutenants include representatives of other terrorist organizations, such as Ayman Al-Zawahiri of Egyptian Islamic Jihad. Below this ruling council are the military, media, and financial subdivisions, which are responsible for worldwide training and operations. Al-Qaeda resources, though dwindling due to destruction and counterterrorism operations, are and have been comprised of training camps, warehouses, communication facilities, and commercial operations.

Among the commercial operations—such as construction companies, mining interests, and agricultural endeavors (including opium)—are several companies that bin Laden started in various countries. Additionally, there are financial and banking businesses, such as the Al Shamal Islamic Bank, whose website listed cooperative banking relationships with institutions in New York, Geneva, Paris, and London.[9]

Al-Qaeda's short-term goals include the removal of U.S. military forces from Saudi Arabia, which is home to Islam's two holiest sites, and the establishment of a Palestinian state. Bin Laden did not originally have a Palestinian state as part of the agenda of al-Qaeda, but has skillfully used that issue in the Middle East to rally support for his own endeavors.[10] Among the long-term goals of al-Qaeda are promoting a worldwide jihad that destroys non-Islamic states and establishes societies, cultures, and states around the globe that will be governed by Islamic law. "One of the most striking innovations of bin Laden's brand of international terrorism has been a vision of a holy war, or jihad, that excludes any possibility of compromise."[11]

In a very real sense, then, the goal of al-Qaeda is not to negotiate with the West, but to eradicate it. Yoni Fighel, a researcher at the Institute for Counter-Terrorism, writes:

> As a cultural struggle, the world-wide Jihad is waged on three fronts. The most immediate front is within Muslim countries, where the goals are to reinstate the rule of *Sharia* law. The second front is in countries with Muslim minorities, situated on "fault lines" with other cultures, such as the Balkans, the Caucasus, Kashmir, etc. And the last front is in the international cultural struggle, in which Islam takes on Western—particularly American—civilization, perceived by the fundamentalists as the source of all evil, and the primary threat to Islam.[12]

While at least 5,000 militants trained in al-Qaeda camps in Afghanistan before the camps were destroyed during Operation Enduring Freedom, it is estimated that more than 50,000 people have been trained in similar camps run by other organizations.[13] Officials in China have even estimated that as many as 1,000 Chinese Muslims have been trained in al-Qaeda camps.[14]

The effort against al-Qaeda will likely continue for months or even years, but it can be successful. However, dead or alive, Osama bin Laden will continue to be a force to be reckoned with for years to come. If bin Laden dies as a martyr, his name will inspire militant Muslims to carry on the struggle for his cause and version of Islam because ideas often live long after their leaders die.

The battle against international terrorism is an ideological war as well as a military one. It will likely continue for years, but the beginning salvos against it are working. Peter L. Bergen states the situation well:

> To borrow an old adage, what goes around comes around. The global nature of al-Qaeda and its affiliated groups is now mirrored by the global effort to contain them in the wake of the September 11, 2001 carnage.... In the past al-Qaeda has carried its holy war from its base in Afghanistan to countries around the world. Now the world is carrying that war back to al-Qaeda.[15]

Anguish in Afghanistan

In Afghan folklore there is a story that recounts the creation of the world. Part of the tale is that when God had finished with His work of creation, he took all the rubble, rock, and refuse that was left over and dumped it one place—Afghanistan.[16] Ideology, history, religion, ethnicity, and economics have all played a part in the current and past struggles for power in Afghanistan. Conflict and war are not new to this part of the world. Afghanistan has been invaded numerous times since Alexander the Great marched his armies into this region in 330 B.C. This "Silk Route" crossroads has been the site of centuries of conflict. When Alexander the Great reached the mountains of the Hindu Kush, he believed that he had reached the farthest limits of the earth. There on the fringes of civilization his armies faced enormous physical and military challenges fighting local tribesmen. In the end, Alexander was victorious, but it came at a high cost in human lives.

A thousand years later, in A.D. 654, Arab armies swept through Afghanistan, bringing with them the new religion of Islam, which quickly took hold in the land. About 500 years later, in 1219, Genghis Khan and his Mongol hordes swept though the land, bringing intermarriage between the Mongols and local tribes and contributing to diversity in the region. Further invasions over the centuries continued to create a linguistic, ethnic, and regional patchwork quilt that blanketed the mountains, desert, and plains of Afghanistan. This rich and complex ethnic, cultural, and religious mix has since always made nation-building very difficult. In a land where local and tribal loyalties far outweigh attempts at a national consciousness, conflict and civil war have been and continue to be inevitable.

In the early 1800s the British made their first contact in the region, and Afghanistan soon became sandwiched between two great empires, the Russian and the British. A pawn in what the West called "the Great Game," brutal conflict in Afghanistan raged throughout the century, culminating in the Third Anglo-Afghan War in 1919.[17] The reputation of the Afghans as ferocious fighters and the land as an arduous place for battle has been one that has endured through the centuries. Long before the Soviet Union invaded in 1979 and lost 40,000 men over the next decade, the British learned the difficulty of fighting in Afghanistan—a reality popularized in the vivid words of Rudyard Kipling:

> When you're wounded and left on Afghanistan's plains
> And the women come out to cut up what remains
> Just roll to your rifle and blow out your brains
> An' go to your Gawd like a soldier.[18]

British journalist Ben MacIntyre writes of this land and its history:

> There is a strange, cruel pattern to Afghan history, where the coup is the accepted method of government transition, and fratricide merely the bluntest form of politics. It is a history of repeated invasion and permanent, chronic instability, compounded by internal tribal, ethnic and religious splits, coupled with an ancient warrior tradition, poverty, ignorance, corruption and multi-generational feuds buried so deep in the past that the roots have long been forgotten.
>
> It is a myth that Afghanistan repels all invaders, for the country has been successively overrun, by Persians, Turks, Greeks, Mongols, Arabs, Moguls, Sikhs, Russians and the British. Rather, it bleeds and baffles the invader until he stumbles home, thwarted by the Afghan mastery of guerilla warfare, political duplicity, immunity to hardship, and skill at forging tribal alliances that evaporate the moment the foreigner is gone. War never ends here, but merely evolves and mutates, always on a local level, sometimes nationally, never simply.[19]

The lessons of which MacIntyre speaks were learned through battle and bloodshed in the 1980s by Russian soldiers. In the aftermath of their retreat, civil war continued in the land with the phenomenon of the Taliban, the Islamic students' movement, appearing in 1994 and taking the country and the world by storm.[20] The Taliban were the products of the religious schools *(madrassahs)* in Pakistan, and they instituted strict social and religious practices and laws throughout the majority of Afghanistan. They brought temporary law and order to the land, but it was a brutal extremism that no one anticipated, and its excesses are now well-known and documented. Journalist and author Robert Kaplan summarizes the Taliban experience well:

> The Taliban embody a lethal combination: a primitive tribal creed, a fierce religious ideology, and the sheer incompetence, naïveté, and cruelty that are begot by isolation from the outside world and growing up amid war without parents. They are also an example of globalization, influenced by imported pan-Islamic ideologies and supported economically by both Osama bin Laden's worldwide terrorist network (for whom they provide a base) and a multibillion-dollar smuggling industry.... [21]

During their rule, the Taliban spread a broad umbrella over Afghanistan, and one of those who came under their protection was Osama bin Laden. While culture, arts, and a rich heritage were marred and eradicated, al-Qaeda's brand of terrorism found a home and flourished. The Taliban not only tolerated bin Laden and al-Qaeda, it encouraged both, and by so doing, assured its own destruction and demise in the first weeks of the war against terrorism after the 9/11 attacks.

Taking out the Taliban—A One-Round Knockout

The pundits' predictions did not come true. Fighting the Taliban in Afghanistan was not a rerun of either Vietnam or the Russian Afghan experience. While it was not without the loss of American lives, the eight-week campaign against the Taliban went much better than was expected. American firepower and technology, special operations forces, and soldiers of the Northern Alliance came together to topple the Taliban.

With the Taliban gone, the political future of Afghanistan is uncertain. While there is broad international support for the new government, the final outcome will rest with the warlords and leaders who now have to lay aside ruthless rivalries for the greater good of the nation. That will not be an easy task in a land where many people forget everything but their grudges and hatreds.

A Battle Without Borders

When the history of America's first war of the twenty-first century is written, Afghanistan and the Taliban may be just the prologue. Soon to be consigned to history's ash heap of tyrants, dictators, and enemies of freedom, the Taliban will likely never be a threat again. Few people will dispute the fact that we have entered a war unlike previous wars our nation has fought. There are, to be sure, similarities, but there are also dissimilarities.

The destruction of the Taliban is not the same as the destruction of al-Qaeda, but it is a first step. If al-Qaeda cells are going to be destroyed, the war must be waged around the world. Somalia, Sudan, Yemen, Iraq, Indonesia, and the Philippines are all countries where al-Qaeda has a strong foothold. Some such nations are sponsors of terrorism, and others sympathize with it. And then there are other terrorist networks and groups that need to be dealt with. Whether the terrorists are eradicated by military force, financial strangulation, or other means, the war will go on. At times it will be visible, but frequently it will be conducted covertly and quietly. It is, in many respects, a battle without borders, but it is not a battle without goals, guidance, and global support.

Military force is not the only appropriate response to terrorism and terrorist acts, but it is a ready and reliable option when needed. As a nation, we must be prepared to support our leaders and our forces in every just endeavor against terrorism in the months and years ahead. And while it's true that waging such a war is costly, we must remember that it's well worth the protection of our freedoms.

Terrorists are people with a cause, who have a global world-view, and who are willing to act on the basis of their beliefs. Their actions are abhorrent, immoral, and unbiblical, but they accurately reflect what is in the heads and hearts of the terrorists. The religiously motivated terrorist is trying to bring some variation of heaven to earth and, in doing so, ends up bringing hell on earth for his victims and survivors. Terrorists have a vision for how they believe individuals, communities, cultures, and countries should act and interact, and it is a distorted perspective that denies freedom, democracy, and human rights to those who come under their rule. They kill innocent people at the same time that they are claiming to be fighting for those same people. If their dream came true, it would be a nightmare for us all.

Christians also have a worldview—a view of how the world is today and how it could be tomorrow. Theologian Carl F. H. Henry writes:

> Ours is a world of staggering changes in which great nations like Britain topple from world supremacy, sleeping nations like China stir themselves awake, and new nations like Israel rise from the dust of past ages.... It is a world in which man has learned to walk in outer space without cosmic dizziness, halt the advent of human life with a capsule, postpone death by a heart transplant, and commute to the moon....But it is also a runaway world in which totalitarian dictators destroy human dignity and rights openly, while democracies do the same things in more subtle ways. Ours is a world in which war has not only gone global but has also taken to the heavens, in which man has split the atom and treated populous cities like Hiroshima to cremation. It is a world running from the random past into the computerized future. Restless of restraints and running from God, it is

a world on rampage, a world gone radical, rebellious, and renegade, and a world resistant to divine authority.[22]

The biblical view of the world is one which understands that the world is shattered and scarred by sin. The effects of the Fall in the Garden of Eden affect not only relations between individuals, but also between nations. Until Jesus Christ physically returns and establishes his millennial kingdom, the world will never be perfect. But it can be better, and Christians are called to work for such progress.

The worldview of the terrorist is one of many competing perspectives in the battle for ideas and values. Values, of course, have consequences. Biblical values put into action will have biblical consequences; unbiblical values will have unbiblical consequences. Christians should be more involved and engaged in changing culture, society, and the status quo than non-Christians. We too are part of a global network. The church of Jesus Christ also calls to a confused and conflicted world. But it calls individuals to righteousness rather than terror, to justice rather than vengeance, and to love rather than selfish ambition.

The Christian worldview is distinctive and should address every facet of life, including politics, international relations, and government.[23] For Christians, the call to discipleship, evangelism, and cultural engagement is clearly set forth in the verses and principles of the Bible. "You can be part of a strategic alliance who take God and moral absolutes and divine truth seriously; you can lead in the renewing of our crumbling society. The cause of justice and peace in society is a noble one, and evangelicals should be in the forefront of it."[24]

Technological Terror
Cyberterrorism and Information Warfare

While the Internet is now so dispersed that a debilitating physical attack is unlikely, an electronic one could destabilize major parts of the USA's communications grid and economy.[1]

Jon Swartz
USA Today

Owning a personal computer is a great thing. Writing papers, articles, and letters, and designing graphics are so much easier than ever before. But still, software and hardware problems can make a personal computer seem like one's own private terrorist. Fortunately, there is normally but one user, and the terrorist remains at your own fingertips. But connect that computer to another computer, and a door is opened to a whole new world that gets wider and wider as more computers are connected together. First we connect with the next room or across the hall, then we connect to a network at our business, then to the Internet and to the world. In so doing, the world also connects to us, opening the electronic window to

117

terrorism and the possibility of what is now called information warfare (IW).

The Birth of the Information Age

How did we get to where we are today with computers, the Internet, and the potential for catastrophic computer terror? The foundation for the conception of the Internet was a Department of Defense 1957 initiative called the Advanced Research Projects Agency (ARPA). The agency's sole responsibility was to ensure that the United States maintained a lead over the Soviets in science and technology. In 1962, the U.S. Air Force hired RAND (a government think tank) to do a study on how the Air Force could maintain command and control of its missiles in the event of a nuclear attack. RAND was asked to design a *decentralized research network* that could survive a nuclear strike so that a counterattack could be made. The computer-based network slowly developed into the ARPANET, with four host universities (Stanford Research Institute; University of California, Los Angeles; University of California, Santa Barbara; and the University of Utah). With it, scientists could share data and access remote computers, but its most popular use quickly became the sending and receiving of personal messages (digital mail or electronic mail). By 1971, the ARPANET had 23 hosts, connecting universities and government research centers across the country. Two years later, the ARPANET was an international program gradually moving away from its military research roots.

The Internet as we know it today became possible in 1982, when a common language for Internet computers was created (TCP/IP). Expanding from four hosts in 1969 to ten million hosts in 1996, the Internet became an electronic network connecting not just a country, but the entire globe.[2] Americans entered an information age that has and will continue to greatly affect the way each of us lives. And since knowledge is power, this tremendous tool for education, economics, and entertainment can also be a weapon for the disgruntled and disenfranchised members of the global family.

The Birth of Cyberterrorism

Within six years after the Internet began to grow it suffered its first saboteur. On November 1, 1988, a program called "Internet Worm" was introduced into the network, temporarily disabling 6,000 of the 60,000 hosts in operation. Issues related to privacy and security quickly became a top concern in the field of computer technology. Soon, terms like *hacker*, *cracker*, and *electronic break-in* became commonplace, and the first counterterrorism agency was created—the Computer Emergency Response Team (CERT).[3] "Just as increasing dependence upon sea trade brought pirates and navies to the oceans, increasing reliance on the microchip and communications networks will attract criminals, terrorists, and the military interest of nations."[4] But is information terrorism—cyberterrorism—a real threat to national security? And are all computer-related crimes acts of terror?

Although computer attacks are disruptive—with computers referred to as weapons of mass *disruption*—should they be equated with chemical, biological, radiological, and nuclear attacks, which involve weapons of mass *destruction?* Does a terrorist's illegal use of a computer make his act one of terror? Let's take a look at various kinds of computer attacks, discuss the impact of these attacks, and put information terrorism in proper perspective.

What Is Information Terrorism?

Since the 9/11 attacks, discussion about the potential for computer-generated terror has been prominent in newspapers and magazines. But is any and all malevolent use of a computer to be understood as terrorism? Such a broad definition of terrorism provokes undue fear and does not take into consideration the different types of motivations that lead to computer crime. More specifically, we need to keep in mind that terrorism is a political crime that attacks the legitimacy and stability of a government through fear and physical violence.

> Political terrorism is the systematic use of actual or threatened physical violence in the pursuit of a political objective, to create a general climate of public fear and destabilize society, and thus influence a population or government policy. Information terrorism is the nexus [i.e., link] between criminal information system fraud or abuse, and the physical violence of terrorism.[5]

Most abuses of computer privacy are ego-driven, attempts at blackmail, or social or political harassment—that is, ordinary theft, fraud, and extortion that have no connection with acts that threaten a society with physical violence.

If legislation against terrorism is going to be effective, then terrorist acts must be clearly defined, especially if such acts are going to receive more stringent punishments. Criminals and terrorists may benefit from the activities of one another, but they are not the same. Criminal charges and terrorist charges should be differentiated (though they may overlap). For example, the coordination of sit-ins and the defacement of websites are not terrorist acts, although they can be very costly and annoying.

However, unless better network security is achieved, the potential for information terrorism *could be* significant, as noted in a recent edition of *Conflict Studies:*

> All major financial transactions, banks, stock exchanges, and economic structures are driven or linked by computer networks. The networks can be penetrated by physically remote terrorists who can destroy popular confidence in a nation's economic system and thereby inflict a different kind of damage and affect more people than conventional terrorists who cause disruptions with poison gas, bombs, or bullets.[6]

Greater measures must be taken to protect America's economic infrastructure. We must be responsive to the kind of disaster that information terrorism can have on an economy. Would terrorists exploit technological vulnerabilities in the world of computers? We believe they would. Bruce Berkowitz, a research fellow at the Hoover Institution on War, Revolution, and Peace, writes:

> During the past several years, military officials have become concerned about the possibility that a foreign adversary might strike at U.S. computers, communications networks, and databases. Although such an "information warfare" (IW) attack could be part of a larger conventional military operation, an adversary might also use it as a warning shot to dissuade the United States from helping an ally abroad or as part of a terrorist campaign.[7]

Pranks, Ploys, and Personal Politics: An Electronic Playground

Modern activists, popularly called "hacktivists," use the Internet to promote their particular political or social bent. Such modern-day activism is cheap. Hacktivists do not need to rent buses or drive hundreds of miles, buy paper for signs, walk down city streets, sit for hours in front of a convention center, or wear out their voices repeating political slogans. Today they can sit at home, download free hacking software off the Internet (directions included), eat a snack, grab a drink, locate the enemy target (website), develop the political or social statement or graphic they want to leave, click, and then gloat over their successful defacing of the site and attempt at changing world opinion.

Most defacements are mild in nature and nothing more than annoyances. Websites quickly remove them, improve their security, and move on. Yet some defacements are more rebellious in nature, taking on an antiauthority angle. For example, a group known as PoisonBox hacked into the Suffern Police Department computer network in New York, where they left a message akin to 1960s graffiti: "Hello boys and girls, always remember: the law is for suckers."[8] Other defacement is hate-based and becomes a tool of hackers engaged in cyberwar. This occurred, for example, between China and Taiwan. Chinese hackers posted messages on Taiwanese and government sites ("Only one China exists and only one China is needed"), while Taiwanese hackers gladly returned electronic blows ("Reconquer, reconquer, reconquer the mainland"). Israeli and Palestinian hackers, and other adversaries around the world, regularly send threatening messages to each other's websites.

Sit-ins are more aggressive cyberattacks. For a sit-in to be successful, tens of thousands of people need to participate. During the 1999 street protests against the World Trade Organization in Seattle, the United Kingdom-based Electrohippies Collective organized the simultaneous visits of users, each of whom pointed their electronic browsers at the heart of the WTO website, creating hundreds of thousands of hits all at once. Their purpose was to overload the system and disrupt normal service.

Another way to interrupt a website's availability is to alter a website's Domain Name Server so that anyone wanting to visit the site is directed to an alternate site. Thus one person can act to deny any access to a target website. A single hacker can also acquire software that will allow him or her to send thousands of messages that eventually overload a service and either cause it to crash or make access to it so difficult that normal traffic eventually fades away. These intrusions are called "denial of service" (DoS) attacks.[9]

A common and well-known type of DoS attack is the virus. Viruses are destructive programs or self-replicating codes created by hackers. They generally come in the form of e-mails or are planted in programs that, when opened, overload, disable, or damage the computer. The hacker does this by determining a shortcoming in a computer program, system, or security setup, and then inserts his virus.

Some have argued that we need to be more aware of the security risks posed by such shortcomings or weaknesses.

"The most significant danger and vulnerability facing the Wired World is continuing to accept and standardize corporate and consumer computer environments on technology *that's proven time and again to be insecure, unstable, and full of documented bugs ("features") that routinely place the Internet community at risk*" (emphasis added).[10] If weaknesses are indeed found, then appropriate action should be taken to prevent the cyberattack from happening again. For example, due to a June 1999 security breach, the U.S. Army changed the service for its website, www.army.mil, from a Microsoft Windows NT-based server to StarNine's WebSTAR Server Suite 4.0, which runs on a Mac operating system. Their purpose in making the move was to provide greater web security.[11]

One way to find potential weaknesses in a computer program or system is to invite hackers to attempt to uncover them. "There is such a thing as white-hat hacking, where large corporations hire the most clever and mischievous of virtual raiders to probe their defenses for weaknesses."[12] Understanding the ways in which hackers can break into a network can help technicians improve Internet security.

Planes, Power Grids, and Processing Plants: An Electronic Power Play

Cyberterrorism is activism (hacktivism) taken to the next level. The terrorists' activism goes beyond words to weapons. Some people believe that terrorists in general are limited to low-tech capabilities because they are poor and uneducated, but the truth is that a good number have significant scientific and technological knowledge, and this knowledge is used to carry on the work of terrorism. "Communication on the Internet facilitates leaderless resistance by allowing leaders of the movement to convey information to sympathizers worldwide without having to meet them face-to-face."[13] Also, it is not difficult to conceal instructions for an upcoming attack in a computer graphic. *Steganography* is the art of hiding into a picture written messages that are too small for the naked eye to read. Terrorists have and do use this tool. "A terrorist could insert plans for blowing up a nuclear reactor in, say, the nose of a puppy on a pet-adoption website."[14] Those receiving the concealed message would not have to be as computer literate as those developing and sending the message.

What about the future? Dorothy Denning at Georgetown University writes, "Cyberspace is increasingly used as a digital battleground for rebels, freedom fighters, terrorists, and others who employ hacking tools to protest and participate in broader conflicts."[15] Computers can be easily used to place messages on the websites of enemies, as a resource for getting information about a potential target, as tutors for the construction of explosive munitions and toxic chemicals, to electronically transfer illegal funds instantaneously around the globe, and to serve as a link between operatives. But to what extent would computers be used to attack a target directly?[16] Concerns about how terrorists might use computers have produced some frightening scenarios:

- Terrorists could cause a mass-casualty plane crash by interfering with the air traffic control system of an airport.[17]

- Terrorists could attack computers at commercial harbor facilities used to ship military supplies, or the air traffic control system supporting movement of military personnel and equipment.[18]

- Terrorists could target commercial suppliers and manufacturers to disrupt production and distribution of military equipment and weapons.[19]

- Terrorists could break into the network of a power company and disable the computers that distribute electricity.

- Terrorists could cause pressure overload in gas lines to disable valves, hoping to create an explosion in a certain portion of a city.

- Terrorists could remotely disrupt the financial infrastructures of major banking institutions or stock exchanges. This would cause a loss of confidence and could create economic panic globally. Some attempts have been somewhat successful—for example, Palestinian hackers penetrated the Bank of Israel and the Israeli Stock Exchange.

- Terrorists could obtain remote-control devices that set off conventional weapons or even weapons of mass destruction. If they could acquire such weaponry, it could make the suicide bomber obsolete.[20]

If terrorist organizations can afford, obtain, and deploy such computer technologies, they would certainly use them.

The following quote appeared in the *San Francisco Chronicle* and was used to support an expert's overdramatized claim that cyberterrorism is the "most insidious type of terrorism."[21] "During the bombing campaign in Kosovo and Serbia in Spring 2000, 100 NATO computer network servers were subjected to continuous e-mail bombings and 'ping' assaults— which tied up network servers by forcing them to respond to repeated requests for information—that effectively shut the NATO machines down for several days."[22] If this is "insidious," what would we call the attacks of 9/11? One cannot equate pings with bombs!

When it comes to cyberterrorism, the possibilities are as far-reaching as people's imaginations and technology are able to take them. However, cyberterrorism is not the greatest terrorist threat we face. In response to the present-day concerns on cyberterrorism, Richard Forno offers some calming insights:

> In the aftermath of our national tragedy [September 11], there is an understandable increase in emotional rhetoric in chat rooms and coffee bars across America that the recent attacks will precipitate a so-called "cyberwar." The "cyberwar" will likely be no more

than the run-of-the-mill nuisances and mundane mischief that network and security administrators see on a daily basis—web defacements, ping floods, virus attacks, and so on. Sadly, there are a growing number of security and "intelligence" vendors making claims that the attacks of September 11 will culminate in or help launch a "cyberwar"; thus creating an unnecessary amount of Fear, Uncertainty, and Doubt (FUD) on a topic that is in no way as pressing a concern as the real emergencies that we are currently facing.[23]

Cyberterrorism may grow into a more significant problem in the future; for now, the main concerns relate to how terrorists use computers to their own advantage. For example, a major problem is the fact that terrorists can use computers to launder money. The ability to quickly move funds around the globe is a key weapon in the terrorist's arsenal. No one knows for sure how much money is laundered each year, but the International Monetary Fund (IMF) estimates that it may be as much as 1.5 trillion dollars, or two to three percent of the global gross domestic product (GDP).[24] Most of that money is being laundered by individual criminals and organized crime, but some of it is done by terrorists. The concern was addressed legally in the International Money Laundering Abatement and Anti-Terrorist Financing Act of 2001, which President Bush signed on October 26, 2001. Part of the ongoing fight against terrorism will be to eliminate or severely hinder the ability to launder money via computers.

Faith & Fear

Throughout the process of creating the heavens and the earth, and upon the completion of creating everything, God pronounced that his creation was good. And not only was it good, it was very good. Only once did God refer to a situation as being "not good" (Genesis 2:18), and this was a condition that he quickly remedied by molding from Adam his perfect match, Eve. Before our first parents exercised their free will and rebelled against God, the state of the earth and the human heart was good, just as God intended them to be. The possibility of terror, though only a decision away, was nowhere in sight. The heavens and the earth and all that they offer were created and given to us for good alone.

But what God intends for good, humanity can use for evil. God chose to create men and women with the freedom to choose God or choose self. When we seek our own way, all that God created for our benefit can then be altered and misused for human gratification and glory. There is a lesson to be remembered here: God wants what is best for humanity; he always has and he always will. From the time Adam and Eve fell victim to their visions of grandeur and self-glory, all the way to the present, God has tirelessly and patiently sought us—to the point of sending Jesus Christ to die for us so that we could return to him, our refuge. "Preserve me, O God, for I take refuge in You. I said to the LORD, 'You are my Lord; I have no good besides You'" (Psalm 16:1-2).

Through a relationship with God, we become reflections of God's goodness and are better able to use science and technology in ways that benefit humanity rather than harm it. Even though weapons may be used for just causes, we must remember that they exist because of evil—they exist because human beings pursue their own direction rather than God's. Ultimately, in God's plan, "He will judge between many peoples and render decisions for mighty, distant nations. Then they will hammer their swords into plowshares and their spears into pruning hooks; nation will not lift up sword against nation, and never again will they train for war. Each of them will sit under his vine and under his fig tree, with no one to make them afraid" (Micah 4:3-4). May we live each day to this end.

What Joseph told his brothers so long ago—"you meant evil against me, but God meant it for good in order to bring about this present result, to preserve many people alive" (Genesis 50:20)—is true to this day. Good can and will come from the terrible tragedy of September 11, 2001; it will certainly come to those who turn to God for comfort and strength rather than with intent to blame.

Goodness is among the foremost attributes of God, and an end to which all who love God and those who rule—whether they submit to his authority or not—must work. His justice and holiness are exercised in part as a response to humanity's intent to cause harm. In the end, God's justice, like discipline, is exercised to bring about a change that leads to good. The murderous attack of 9/11 was not an attack by God against infidels; it was a brutal attempt to force an errant theological message on others. It was an act contrary to God's character. A just and decisive response to such evil is the responsibility of a good government:

> Rulers are not a cause of fear for good behavior, but for evil. Do you want to have no fear of authority? Do what is good and you will have praise from the same; for it [government] is a minister of God to you for good. But if you do what is evil, be afraid; for it does not bear the sword for nothing; for it is a minister of God, an avenger who brings wrath on the one who practices evil (Romans 13:3-4).

Government's primary responsibility, then, is to promote justice for all of its citizens.

What terrorists and rogue nations do to cause evil will, in ways yet unknown, be used by God to bring about good. In the meantime, it is the responsibility of Christian citizens to participate passionately and peacefully in all areas of American life: political, social, economic, and academic. Our goal should be to influence for good, not to set up a Christian state. The establishing of governments is God's business; he is sovereign over all that happens with leaders and nations. And ultimately, even with the evil that's rampant in our world, we can have full confidence that God is good, and we as Christians are called to reflect his goodness to the watching world around us.

Toxic Terror

"Bugs and Gas"

Without a shadow of a doubt there is something in man's makeup that causes him to hesitate when at the point of bringing war to his enemies by poisoning him or his cattle and crops or spreading disease. Even Hitler drew back from this.[1]

Vannevar Bush, 1949
Wartime Science Advisor to Franklin D. Roosevelt

What is deadly, relatively cheap and easy to make, fairly simple to conceal, and the great equalizer between the super-haves and the have-nots? The answer: biological and chemical weapons (BCW). The belief articulated by Vannevar Bush in the above quote is a hopeful one, but not one supported by the facts of human nature and history. Terrorists bent on murdering as many people as possible—by any means that becomes available to them—have taken Americans back to a time that our ancestors knew, a time when diseases like smallpox and plague were personal concerns.

Triple Play and It's Over

Out #1

The idea that people would use biological or chemical weapons ("bugs and gas," BCW) against fellow human beings may be difficult for most Americans to accept. But recent events have forced us to a rather grim reality. America's widely held belief in the basic goodness of human beings is under review. When asked what type of terrorist attack might take place within 12 months of the September 11 attacks, 53 percent stated that the use of BCW was a genuine possibility.[2]

Out #2

It is not only a more correct understanding of human nature that dispels the belief that the worst among us will shy away from using BCW. History overwhelmingly contradicts the perspective of this chapter's opening quote. In fact, the use of BCW in warfare has been fairly regular through the ages.

- 1000 B.C.—Chinese soldiers used arsenical smokes (chemical warfare, CW).

- 424 B.C.—The Spartans used noxious smoke and flames against Athenian-allied cities during the Peloponnesian Wars (CW).

- 1346—Tartar soldiers catapulted the bodies of plague victims over the walls at Kaffa (modern Feodossia in Ukraine). Some historians believe that this action created a pandemic (disease that is prevalent throughout an entire country or continent) that spread through Europe (biological warfare, BW).

- 1710—Russians attempted to spread disease among their Swedish enemies with plague-infested cadavers (BW).

- 1767—The British are believed to have decimated Indians loyal to the French by giving them blankets infected with the smallpox virus (BW).

- 1864—Confederate soldiers killed animals and left them to rot in ponds to deny General Sherman's army adequate supplies of water (BW).

- 1915—Germans deployed 168 tons of chlorine gas in multiple attacks against Allied troops at Ypres, Belgium. This attack is said to be the first *major* use of chemical agents in modern warfare (CW).

- 1918—Germans fired phosgene and chloropicrin projectiles against Americans near Bios de Remieres, France, giving Americans their first experience with a gas attack (CW).

- 1937–1945—The Japanese developed a biological weapons factory in Manchuria, China, running tests on local citizens and prisoners of war. In 1940, an epidemic of bubonic plague was caused when Japanese planes dropped grain and infected fleas. The rats attracted by the grain came in contact with the fleas, and the rats, in turn, acted as carriers of the disease to the human population (BW).

- 1945—The Germans contaminated a Bohemian reservoir with raw sewage (BW).[3]

The historical evidence suggests that some human beings will use whatever is available to inflict damage on an enemy. From 1979 to 1988 Iraq used mustard gas to inflict nearly 5,000 deaths and 45,000 injuries upon enemies.[4] Thus, to suggest that a nation or a nonstate entity (e.g., terrorists, mercenaries, criminals) will not use BCW is naïve. In warfare, the strategy of some will be to use any means available to overcome the enemy.

Out #3

Besides incorrect beliefs about the nature of human beings and the historical record, there is a third error supporting the hope that BCW will not be employed. The ban on biological weapons at the 1972 Biological Weapons and Toxins Conference and the ban on chemical weapons at the 1993 Chemical Weapons Convention led people to hope that the resources and know-how required to develop and deploy BCW would prevent additional nations from acquiring BCW capability. But three decades after the Biological Weapons and Toxins Conference, this has changed. Iraq, Iran, Syria, Libya, China, North Korea, and possibly Sudan, Pakistan, and Kazakhstan, along with eight other nations, have been added to the list of those possessing biological weapons, and many additional nations also have chemical weapons programs as well.

Similarly, to suppose that terrorists do not have the technological capability to develop and produce weapons of mass destruction is wrong. According to a recent *Time* article, "A far more virulent strain of the bacterium called 0157:H7 [a stronger and more effective strain of the *Escherchia coli* (*E. coli*)]…is beyond the technical capabilities of most terrorists."[5] Obviously, however, the fact that terrorists do not possess a particular capability this year does not mean that they will not successfully develop that capability in the future. In the conclusion of his book *Toxic Terror*, Jonathan B. Tucker suggests that historical shortcomings in the use of BCW negate the likelihood of success in the future: "only a tiny minority of terrorists will seek to inflict indiscriminate fatalities, and few if any of them will succeed."[6] But, how many terrorists does it take to create an epidemic? Failure in the past does not mean failure in the future. Perpetrators of mass casualty attacks may have not typically opted for unconventional weapons in the past, but they may in the future.[7]

While there is growing awareness and concern about biological terrorism,[8] some Americans believe that the hurdles standing between terrorists and the use of BCW are still quite formidable. "There is an underappreciation of the technological obstacles to delivery, particularly with biological weapons."[9] However, Bill Patrick (a scientist and leader of America's offensive and defensive bioweapons program from 1951 to 1986 and an Iraqi weapons inspector in 1994) has described how "a terrorist could mount a germ attack on the World Trade Center using a blender, cheesecloth, a garden sprayer, and some widely available hospital supplies."[10] Americans have no time for complacency.

We felt safer before the events of December 7, 1941, and of September 11, 2001, and after both incidents, we prayed that we would never again allow ourselves to fall into a sense of false security. To succeed in this, we must not fail to respect the natural human tendency that lies within each of us to commit evil acts (out #1); nor ignore the historical realities of human conflict (out #2); nor place our confidence in the belief that BCW technology is beyond the reach of those willing to use it against us (out #3). Kanatjan Alibekov (Ken Alibek), a Russian physician, bioweaponeer, and deputy chief of Russia's BCW program Biopreparat from 1988 to 1992 (and who defected to the United States in 1992) warns the world of potential danger:

> The threat of a biological attack has increased as the knowledge developed in our labs—of lethal formulations that took our scientists years to discover—has spread to rogue regimes and terrorist groups. Bioweapons are no longer contained within the bipolar world of the Cold War.[11]

Bugs and Gas: Just the Facts

Why would anyone develop biological and chemical weapons? From the development of the club to the development of thermonuclear technology, political and religious activists and nations have shown a propensity to expand their will through the power of death and destruction. But after the development of nuclear weapons, nations began to think in terms of killing large groups of people without destroying infrastructure (buildings, streets, bridges, etc.).[12] This certainly makes sense; the advantages of not having to rebuild are obvious. However, terrorists are not interested in protecting infrastructure; they are interested in any means that will bring about the deaths of those whom they hate. For them, BCW is a cost-effective means of spreading misery and death. The following is a general overview of what BCW are available and the threats they impose.

Biological Weapons

These are inherently offensive weapons of mass destruction that harness and deploy living organisms to destroy human beings as well as their animals and crops. These weapons consist of pathogens (disease-causing organisms—mostly bacteria and viruses) or toxins (poisons of biological origin). Though the microbial world consists of millions of species, it is only those that are pathogenic and toxic that interest bioweaponeers. Once an organism is harnessed, a proper delivery system has to be developed. The best system for the widely recognized candidates is one that can disperse the pathogen with aerosols. Currently, it is this effective aerosolization which is the terrorist's technological challenge.

- *Bacillus anthracis.* Anthrax is the most recognized lethal bacteria in America. We started hearing about it in the media during the Gulf War. The military believed that Saddam Hussein had produced tons of this material and was willing to deploy it on the battlefield. Anthrax is a bacterium that is deadly to hoofed animals. It is released back to soil from infected animal carcasses and remains stable in the environment for years. It is stable because it is able to grow a spore (the resting or dormant stage of a bacterium) that protects it from the elements until it enters a suitable environment in which it can germinate and spread. A person can inhale the spores through the nose or mouth (*inhalation* anthrax), ingest them by eating contaminated food (*intestinal* anthrax), or get them into the bloodstream through the skin (*cutaneous* anthrax). Inhalational symptoms begin in a few days with flu-like symptoms followed by fever, weakness and discomfort, a cough, and mild chest discomfort. It is in the early stages of infection that medical treatment is most effective. Later symptoms include breathing difficulties, perspiration, and a bluish coloring of the skin caused by a deficiency of oxygen. Shock and death occur within 24 to 36 hours of the onset of the more severe symptoms. Infection in the skin is the least fatal of the three forms. Cutaneous anthrax creates lesions that are usually painless, but if they are left untreated, they may progress to septicemia (the disease getting into the bloodstream) and death. Inhalation and intestinal anthrax are more difficult to cure, but vaccines and medications are available and effective if administered before symptoms are present. Russia has developed a strain of the disease that is resistant to five antibiotics.[13]

• *Yersinia pestis.* The plague is one of humanity's greatest killers. An attack of bubonic plague does not last long, but its murderous toll can be frightening. In A.D. 262, the disease ravaged Rome, killing many thousands. In the fourteenth century, Crusaders carried the disease to Europe, and a quarter of its population died. And at the height of the Great Plague in London (1665), 7,000 people died each week. Plague has traditionally been transmitted to human beings by fleas from infected rats. Once the carrier was identified, strict quarantines and the extermination of rats helped to limit the spread of plague. Today, international agreement requires that any outbreak in the world be given worldwide publicity.

Symptoms of bubonic plague begin after a one- to eight-day incubation period. Local abscesses develop that form painful lumps (buboes), particularly in the neck, armpits, and groin regions. Patients experience chills and fever, headaches, and, if left untreated, shock, delirium, organ failure, and death. In some naturally occurring cases, the disease may be transmitted from one person to another by nothing more than a sneeze or a cough. This is known as pneumonic plague and is the most severe form of the disease. It has an incubation period of two to three days. The disease infects the bronchial system and produces a fatal attack of pneumonia that fills the lungs with fluid and thereby prevents oxygen from reaching the body's organs. A toxin that is released by the plague bacteria when the body's immune system attempts to fight the disease eventually attacks the circulatory system. Convulsions, delirium, and coma sometimes precede death. Biological warfare would likely employ aerosols, hence cases would be pneumonic.

Antibiotics can be quite effective in treating pneumonic plague if administered early in the course of the disease. A vaccine regimen was also available in the past, although it offers no protection against aerosol exposure. In the event of an aerosol attack or if the disease is acquired by means of a cough, the antibiotic doxycycline is administered. But what if scientists develop a new strain that is resistant to antibiotics? Because of its lack of stability in the environment, U.S. bioweapons developers lost interest in plague as an offensive weapon. The Russians were not so easily discouraged. "Plague can be grown easily in a wide range of temperatures and media, and we eventually developed a plague weapon capable of surviving in an aerosol while maintaining its killing capacity. In the city of Kirov, we maintained a quota of twenty tons of plague in our arsenals every year."[14]

• Other pathogens considered for use as biological weapons include: smallpox; camelpox, which Iraq may be developing;[15] tularemia; Q Fever; botulinum toxin; ricin toxin; Venezuelan equine encephalitis; Marburg virus (this insidious killer was identified in 1967 in Germany and is called "liquid death" because it liquefies the body's organs—the corpses of its victims are literally wet with blood); Ebola virus, Russian spring-summer encephalitis; Bolivian hemorrhagic fever (Machupo); Argentinean hemorrhagic fever (Junin); dengue fever; and Lassa fever. "Based on our current level of knowledge, at least seventy different types of bacteria, viruses, rickettsiae, and fungi can be weaponized."[16]

Disease is a ferocious natural enemy, and it just keeps coming back. While pesticides, immunizations, and sanitation have been used to control many diseases, in recent years, doctors have noticed an unsettling trend. Patients are coming to them with bacteria that are resistant to antibiotics. "What they were witnessing was the fast and furious pace of microbiological evolution, sped up in response to a human-modified environment."[17] Basically, bacteria are adapting to survive, and in doing so, may become more virulent by developing resistance to antibiotic treatments previously used against them. This is threat enough; however, human beings can increase the threat via abuses of biotechnology.

Biotechnology in the form of genetic engineering has made it possible to create antibiotic-resistant pathogens and to slice a viral genome (genetic blueprint) of one pathogen and then knit it together with another (known as recombinant DNA) to make a chimera virus (e.g., smallpox-Marburg or smallpox-Ebola).[18] The illness resulting from exposure to such a virus might end up being identified and treated as being caused by one component, while the other component goes undiagnosed long enough to do incredible harm.

One of the great advantages of medical advances and scientific knowledge is that we can use them to protect and prolong life and keep diseases at bay. Unfortunately, there are some who use these advances and developments to perpetrate death.

> Genetic engineering and genomics portend a brave new world. By laying bare blueprints of all life, science—legitimate and otherwise—will create new forms of life and modify existing ones in countless ways. With respect to biological warfare, in theory microbiologists can engineer genes for antibiotic resistance, increased human virulence, or specific and multiple toxins into any number of microbes or higher forms of life. By isolating and cloning virulence factors weapon designers could transform common, innocuous bacteria into pathogenic agents.[19]

Biological agents, available now or in the future, make convenient terrorist weapons because they are easily concealed and transported. And, before the effect of an attack is noticed, a terrorist can be far from the scene of the crime.

Chemical Weapons

"Scientific advancement, especially in the chemical industry, means that a greater variety of inflammable and highly toxic chemicals are commonplace in factories throughout the world. Moreover, by facilitating both cross-border communication and access to information, the Internet enables small groups of dedicated terrorists to operate globally."[20] On March 20, 1995, a chemical weapon was deployed not on a battlefield but against the general population. As we read earlier in this book, a small group of religious radicals in Japan (Aum Shinrikyo), bent on bringing on an apocalypse, expanded the arsenal of the terrorist to include chemical weapons. The group deployed Sarin gas in a Tokyo subway station, killing 12 people and injuring 1,000 more. With the spread of the pesticide, petro-chemical, fertilizer, and pharmaceutical industries throughout the world, any country or group with access to such industries "has the potential in terms of equipment, raw materials, warfare, and technical expertise to produce some chemical agents."[21] Unless these industrial plants are closely monitored, their products could end up being used not only for commercial purposes (eliminate your insect problems), but for military purposes as well (eliminate you).

Chemical weapons are quite different from biological weapons. Rather than living microorganisms or their toxins (poisons) extracted from living organisms, chemical weapons are man-made toxic agents, most of which are liquid or gas that can be dispersed with a sprayer or by munitions, or are "absorbed onto a fine talcum-like powder to create 'dusty agents.'"[22] While many biological weapons have a two- to ten-day incubation period (the time between infection and when physical signs of infection are visible), chemical weapons affect their victims within minutes or hours (among biological weapons, toxins such as botulinum, staph, and ricin have immediate effects also).

The value of a chemical agent is measured by its persistency (how long it remains in the area in which it is dispensed) and effectiveness (how much damage it causes in that area). Chemical weapons are basically divided into two categories: 1) *casualty agents*—nerve agents, blister agents, choking agents (or lung-damaging agents), and blood agents, all of which are intended to severely immobilize or kill their victims; and 2) *riot-control* or *incapacitating agents*—tearing agents, vomiting agents, and psychochemical agents, which incapacitate people with unpleasant effects or cause confusion, hallucination, and delirium.[23]

Though chemical weapons may not be as easy to conceal as biological weapons due to differences in weight and size and the amounts necessary to affect equal areas of impact (a few kilograms of anthrax, when dispensed properly, can cause an equal amount of casualties as a metric ton of Sarin),[24] with good planning, they can be used effectively to create terror, excruciating pain, and death.

In 1987, the United States was the only publicly declared state capable of conducting chemical warfare. Today, the list of nations that possess or have the ability to develop chemical weapons includes the Balkan states, Bulgaria, Burma, China, the Czechoslovakian states, Egypt, Ethiopia, France, Hungary, Indonesia, Iran, Iraq, Israel, Laos, Libya, North Korea, Romania, Russia, South Africa, Syria, Taiwan, and Vietnam.[25] As the list continues to grow even longer, so also grows the threat to America.

- *Vesicants* or *Blister Agents.* The Germans used sulfur mustard in World War I. Though the gas caused few fatalities, the casualties were extensive. The main effect of sulfur mustard and Lewisite is insidious blistering of the skin and of the lining of all bodily passages that are open to the air (mucous membranes). It creates tremendous irritation in the eyes; can extensively damage the lungs; and, if ingested, destroys the lining of the stomach, causing massive fluid loss. Though initial contact with the agent on the skin is indiscernible in the first few hours, incapacitating blisters develop within 12 to 24 hours. Death is rare, but recovery can take from 1 to 4 months (Lewisite blisters heal within several weeks).[26]

- *Nerve Agents.* Dr. Gerhard Schrader accidentally discovered these awful killers in 1930 while attempting to develop a stronger insecticide. His first creation was Tabun (GA), which was followed two years later by

Sarin (GB). Sarin suffocates its victims by paralyzing the chest muscles. Death can take place in as little as 15 minutes. "It is 26 times more deadly than cyanide gas and is 20 times more lethal than potassium cyanide."[27] But nothing compares to its later cousin, VX ("V" denotes its low volatility and long persistence—unlike Sarin, cyanide, and its "G" cousins, VX does not vaporize quickly; it remains on exposed surfaces for a long time). A more adhesive and thickened form of the agent can remain toxic and on the ground for three to four weeks, depending upon weather conditions.

When a person comes into contact with VX in its liquid form, the body absorbs the agent through the eyes or the skin. The lethal effect takes place anywhere from five minutes to 18 hours later. If a victim inhales the gaseous form, symptoms and death are almost immediate (seconds to minutes). The agent cripples the enzyme that transmits signals to the nerves. This inhibition causes various effects such as blurred vision, difficulty in breathing, nausea, vomiting, impaired judgment, loss of consciousness, convulsive seizures, muscular weakness, and respiratory failure.[28]

Saddam Hussein's use of chemical weapons in 1984 against Iran and again in 1988 against the Kurds in his own country strongly suggests that he is willing to use them if the opportunity presents itself. In the years after the Gulf War, a U.N. inspection team found documents in Iraq confirming their suspicions. They discovered that Iraq had produced a VX gas that is ten times more toxic than Sarin. Although the team "destroyed 28,000 chemical weapons, 480,000 liters of chemicals used to make them, and 1.8 million liters of other chemicals,"[29] some analysts suggest that Iraq still has hundreds of tons of chemicals and the technology to produce an even more toxic VX gas.

- *Choking* and *Blood Agents.* The best-known choking agents are phosgene and diphosgene. Within four hours of exposure to these agents, abnormal fluid accumulation in the lungs causes death from suffocation. Phosgene was a World War I chemical warfare agent; it is now widely used in industry. Blood agents include hydrogen cyanide and cyanogen chloride. Cyanide prevents the normal use of oxygen in the organs and tissues of the body. Low amounts of cyanide in the body cause headaches, weakness, disorientation, and nausea; higher amounts cause seizures and respiratory and cardiac failure.[30]

Will weapons like these ever be used against America? Even if every nation in the world bans the use of chemical weapons, there will always be those (like Iraq, who is a signatory against the use of chemical weapons) who will persist in the development of such weapons, and who will perhaps use them. America must stay alert and must remain strong and committed to defending its interests, or it will suffer for its failure. In summary, there are two errors to be avoided in regard to biochemical weapons: The first is the assumption that terrorists can't use them. Such a belief misunderstands the capabilities of terrorists. The second is the assumption that terrorists won't use them. This misunderstands their desire. Both assumptions are wrong.

Faith & Fear

The military concern that changes in wind direction during the delivery of BCW agents in open warfare will bring incapacitation and death to one's own forces is of no concern to the terrorist. Whether in Jerusalem or New York City, the mission of a suicide bomber is to die for his cause while taking as many of the enemy as possible. If dispersing a chemical in the lobby of a building can terrorize the enemy more than an explosion, why not spread the chemical agent and then blow yourself up? Think of the potential damage a person could cause in a big city as a carrier of smallpox. If a person believes that God will be honored by martyrdom and by bringing death to infidels, then self-sacrifice becomes worthwhile.

These are the words of the terrorist and murderer Mohammed Atta, which were found among his belongings after his attack at the World Trade Center on September 11: "Everybody hates death, fears death. But only those, the believers who know the life after death and the reward after death, would be the ones who will be seeking death." Compare his words to the words of Moses, found in the Old Testament: "I call heaven and earth to witness against you today, that I have set before you life and death, the blessing and the curse. So choose life in order that you may live, you and your descendants, by loving the LORD your God, by obeying His voice, and by holding fast to Him; for this is your life and the length of your days" (Deuteronomy 30:19-20). Mohammed Atta wants us to believe that God would have us choose a curse over a blessing; a curse that would not only affect the life of the individual who kills himself, but also that person's descendants. Who could do such an evil thing to himself or to those whom he loves? Life is a gift from God. A person who has a legitimate relationship with God chooses life. In whatever way death comes to a Christian, it is clear that it must not come by one's own hand.

Submission to God also excludes the murder of innocent people. When God legislated the command not to murder, he included those labeled as infidels by religious terrorists. It is a universal decree designed to protect all people. And nothing more clearly supports the value of human life than Christ willingly giving up his life for anyone who willingly accepts his death as their own. We die in Christ so that we might live to show others the way, the truth, and the life.

Thinking the Unthinkable
Radiological and Nuclear Nightmares

1975: If terrorists were to employ radioactive contaminants, they could not halt the continuing effects of their act, not even long after they may have achieved their ultimate political objectives. It has not been the style of terrorists to kill hundreds or thousands. To make hundreds or thousands of persons terminally ill would be even more out of character.[1]

Brian M. Jenkins
Terrorist Expert

2001: If we had possessed [nuclear weapons], we would not have waited to use them.[2]

Salam Zaeef
Taliban Ambassador to Pakistan

Times and technology have changed. More and more religiously motivated terrorists have gradually come to overshadow their politically motivated peers with bullets and bomb attacks. The time of "shock attacks" against a few to influence many has passed; in its place is a time of mass

145

casualty attacks against as many as possible. Over the past two decades, religiously motivated groups throughout the world have shown their willingness to impose their ideals by more deadly means. Accessibility to terrorist tactics in both print and computer formats, plans for the construction of bombs on the Internet, improved technology, and Russian scientists in need of jobs after the Cold War have increased the likelihood of rogue nations and terrorists acquiring, planning, and executing even more catastrophic and deadly attacks.

A Bigger Bang

Throughout the history of the world, peace has not been the norm. Regrettably, the norm has been and continues to be war. The history of humanity and the history of science and technology demonstrate that if something negative can be done, it generally will be. "Someday, possibly quite soon, the world will wake up to face a rogue regime or a bunch of terrorists with a nuclear bomb and the will to use it."[3]

Capability, opportunity, and motivation enable an individual to act on his or her beliefs. If those beliefs are good, the world will be the better because of them; if the beliefs are evil, the world will be the worse because of them.

The question then arises: But won't nuclear attacks cause insurmountable damage? Historically, nations with nuclear capabilities have not attacked one another precisely because the damage they could inflict on each other would effectively eliminate both powers, or because a smaller nation's preemptive strike would bring about its own demise. Initiating a nuclear strike, then, would be suicidal. For example, Iraq's use of a nuclear weapon against the United States or its allies would result in a retaliatory attack that would virtually eliminate the Iraqi nation. But how would the United States retaliate against a nuclear attack by a terrorist organization that is dispersed throughout the world? Nonstate terrorists who roam from nation to nation know that they are more difficult to isolate. If they are located, small arms or precision-guided weapons can be used against them without bringing harm to others, whereas a nuclear response would be too broad and therefore much more difficult to justify.

Given the difficulty of responding symmetrically (one for one) to a nuclear terrorist attack, who, then, might a terrorist organization consider the best target? Israel's geographic size and proximity to Arab and Muslim peoples certainly make an attack with radiological and nuclear devices counterproductive. However, the size and location of the United States makes it the perfect target. From coast to coast and within its many skylines are millions of Americans who, some believe, need to understand the tremendous power of Allah. Consider these words from Osama bin Laden: "We don't consider it a crime if we tried to have nuclear, chemical, biological weapons. If I have indeed acquired these weapons, then I thank God for enabling me to do so."[4] To the extent that they might care about such things, there are very few places in the United States that would cause Islamic radicals, or any others, to discuss concerns about collateral damage. September 11 has made one thing clear: America is a "killing field" for Islamic extremists. And if it is true for them, then for whom else might it be true?

Most indigenous terrorists groups operating in the United States are intensely antigovernment and dedicated to racial purity. Though there are no certainties among extremists beyond hatred, it seems unlikely that American militia groups would use radiological or nuclear weapons. Their primary interests are state and federal governments and racial and ethnic minorities. Attacks utilizing weapons that reach out beyond their identified targets would not serve their purposes and would increase the level of public opinion against them. Still, these groups bear watching, since the actions resulting from their fears may threaten peace and freedom.[5]

One Man's Waste Is Another Man's Weapon

The worst type of radiological explosion is one that thrusts together two "subcritical masses of highly processed radioactive material."[6] The collision of two such materials produces a devastating release of energy known as a nuclear blast. But there is another type of nuclear weapon that is now considered a threat to national security, though its "blast" is nothing in comparison to what we normally think of when we envision a nuclear disaster. This type of weapon has been dubbed "the Dirty Bomb."

Such a bomb is relatively easy to make. A terrorist surrounds a conventional weapon (TNT, dynamite, Semtex) with radiological waste, such as might be found at hospitals and industrial facilities or nuclear reactor sites. The deadly conventional explosion distributes dangerous radiological particles throughout the target area. Such bombs have already been built and deployed by Chechen separatists in Chechnya and Moscow. Bin Laden associate Ramzi Yousef may have tried to find radioactive waste to use in his 1993 World Trade Center bomb, and the al-Qaeda network certainly has such desires.[7]

The fatality rate beyond that caused by the initial explosion of a dirty bomb would be dependent upon the type of radioactive material used in the bomb. If the explosive were surrounded by nonlethal levels of medical or industrial radioactive waste (alpha rays), the effect of the radiation would be less because its particles don't easily penetrate the body. However, if a bomb included waste particles from a nuclear reactor's spent fuel rods (gamma rays), the death toll would be more significant. Also, beyond the immediate effects of the bomb, people exposed to the radioactive fallout would have a greater risk of developing premature cancers. People who were fortunate enough to be in their homes at the time of a dirty bomb attack that emitted alpha particles would be fairly safe if they knew and were able to immediately shut down their ventilation systems.

A traditional nuclear blast could potentially kill more than 100,000 people; a dirty bomb might kill hundreds or thousands. Although a dirty bomb might not result in many tens of thousands of casualties, "contamination in small quantities could have major psychological and economic effects."[8] And a dirty bomb is much cheaper, easier, and faster to acquire than other nuclear weapons and some biological and chemical weapons.

The pre-September 11 security on radiological waste at hospitals and industrial facilities was deficient, which increases the likelihood of such material getting into the wrong hands. Internationally, there exists a thriving black market in these materials: "In the past eight years, the U.N.'s International Atomic Energy Agency in Vienna has documented 376 examples of illicit sells [sic] of nuclear wastes and radioactive materials, including 175 in former Soviet territories."[9]

Though the dirty bomb has been scrapped as a military option by the United States and Iraq, it is an affordable option for terrorists, and one that is more readily obtainable. Terrorists can do greater damage by adding radioactive material to their present conventional arsenal. "Even if the terrorists used a crude dissemination device or a quantity of radioactive material too small to present a serious threat to health, fear of radiation could cause panic."[10] Though there is danger in the handling of radioactive materials, this inconvenience can be overcome with training. "Perhaps the most immediate danger is bin Laden's own burning ambition—particularly his desire to launch apocalyptic terrorist attacks on the West—and the close links he has formed recently with Saddam Hussein."[11]

Have Bomb, Will Travel

Imagine a man in a business suit walking with an attaché case, apparently on his way to work. It's early in the morning, and he leaves the apartment where he has lived for several months and walks toward Wall Street. From there he goes to a location near the New York Stock Exchange. Unnoticed, he places the attaché case just inside a magazine stand as the vender works with another customer. One block away he steps into a waiting car that takes him over the Brooklyn Bridge, then west across the Verrazano Bridge and out onto Staten Island. Suddenly, a roaring nuclear blast goes off in New York City. From its point of origin, 150 yards of sheer terror goes out in all directions. The southerly winds send the radioactive fallout toward New Jersey. Whether the terrorist in New York failed to avoid the explosion or escaped, he is a hero of the new world order. This may sound like a sinister plot for a movie, but it could just as easily be a plot for a terrorist attack.

Initial attempts by al-Qaeda in 1993 failed to produce the desired nuclear intercontinental missiles and uranium for which bin Laden had hoped. He turned his focus on a less-powerful weapon, but one that was definitely more powerful than anything he had used before: atomic demolition munitions or nuclear "suitcase bombs."

It is believed that the Soviet Union developed this type of weapon during the Cold War for possible use within the United States by its special forces or spies within the United States. Bin Laden paid the Chechen Mafia in cash and heroin to acquire one of these weapons. General Aleksandr Lebed, former head of President Yeltsin's Security Council, has stated that many of these suitcase bombs are unaccounted for (of 132 weapons, there are 84 missing).[12] American intelligence believes that the Taliban or al-Qaeda may have gained possession of several suitcase bombs in 1998 and stored them somewhere near Kandahar, Afghanistan. Still, detonation of the devices may require Soviet-era codes that are not available to those who currently possess the bombs. However, with the number of discontented and financially hurting former Soviet Special Forces members, it is possible for someone who knows the codes to be recruited to solve that dilemma.[13]

Soviet Dis-Union

For decades, America fought the Cold War with the Soviet Union, the world's other great superpower. The Soviet Union's intercontinental missiles and nuclear submarine fleet were a constant concern to U.S. military and intelligence agencies. Finally, the reforms of Gorbachev, begun in 1984, and the dismantling of the Berlin Wall on November 9, 1989, forced the Soviet Union to gradually dissolve into separate and independent states. The world rejoiced, and there was hope for better and more prosperous days in many places. They seemed inevitable, at least, in the West. However, change was not going smoothly in the Soviet Union. The failure of communist ideology and the breakdown of its military infrastructure left the nation in disrepair economically and socially. The expansive Union of Soviet Socialist Republics had become a dis-Union.

The secession of states created greater poverty in Daghestan and Ingushetia, and ethnic wars flared between Chechnya and Russia, between Armenia and Azerbaijan, and between Georgia and Abkhasia. In the confusion, organized crime and terrorist groups emerged. "Following the breakdown of the communist system, Russia became the most widely discussed and the most important center of organized crime in the world. The extent of Russian army and police corruption is virtually unprecedented."[14] Russia's present condition not only threatens its own future, but potentially, the stability of the world.

One of the largest nuclear weapons arsenals in the world is now open to corruption and theft. "The most obvious symptoms of chaos are corrupt generals selling weapons abroad, inadequately policed borders, and poorly secured facilities housing weapons and their components. The most significant threats to U.S. national security now arise not from Russia's military might, but from its weakness."[15]

On December 7, 2001, Russian authorities reported that they had arrested seven men from the Balashikha crime gang who were attempting to sell two pounds of highly enriched weapons-grade uranium for $30,000. Though this amount is insufficient to make a nuclear weapon, repeated purchases of small amounts could add up to a serious threat. For terrorists and criminals, obtaining radioactive material in small increments is far safer and more likely to be successful, as the transactions are less likely to be noticed. "If confirmed, the seizure would be the first acknowledged case of theft of weapons-grade material in Russia."[16]

Numerous thefts in Russia have involved low-grade uranium that could be used in the making of dirty bombs. Although the United States is assisting Russia by installing fences and surveillance sensors around Russia's more than 1,000 tons of plutonium and uranium, Russian law enforcement will require ongoing support not only to eliminate terrorists, but also to get rid of organized crime groups, "which could make big profits selling nuclear materials to willing buyers."[17]

Russia should be assisted in providing security at its nuclear sites and in developing a program to eliminate its excess plutonium. It is important that Russia does not fail as a democracy as have some nations in the Middle East. The security of her weapons of mass destruction and the safety of the world may rest in the moral strength of Russia's new republic. Though economic and structural reforms are important to Russia's survival, Kanatjan Alibekov, codeputy of the Soviet Union's biological and chemical war machine from 1988 to 1992, reminds us that "what is needed in Russia is moral reform, and until that happens, Russia will not change."[18]

Down but Not Out

These days, the greatest threat of an atomic-type nuclear attack against the United States is from Iraq. Saddam Hussein has continued to be a major concern in world affairs since the Gulf War. There have been repeated difficulties in assessing his production and stockpiling of weapons of mass destruction. Although Israel destroyed an Iraqi reactor in 1981 that was built to produce fissile material for nuclear bombs, some have speculated that Iraq may have continued to produce highly enriched uranium in centrifuges that could operate in underground bunkers. Whether Saddam Hussein is producing it or buying it, researchers estimate that Iraq "is at least five years away from enriching enough uranium for an a-bomb, but could assemble one 'within weeks' of obtaining the material on the black market."[19] His most likely targets are either Israel or the United States. All he has to do is find a way to transport the bomb, and there are plenty of options if an intercontinental cruise missile is unavailable.

Also, as discussed earlier, al-Qaeda has tried—and can be expected to continue to try—to acquire materials for weapons of mass destruction as long as they have the funds and ability. Whether bin Laden lives or dies in this present war on terrorism, he sees it as his "duty to possess the weapons that would prevent the infidels from inflicting harm on Muslims."[20] Hopefully, bin Laden and Saddam Hussein have misinterpreted the hopes, attitudes, and views of the greater Muslim world.

Another regional concern is Iran, which is building a Russian-type reactor in the port city of Bushehr, and a third region of concern is Pakistan. If Pakistan's government should weaken or fall, the nation's nuclear arsenal could easily get into the wrong hands. As has been done in Russia, the United States needs to assist Pakistan in securing its nuclear arsenal and continuing to keep human and electronic eyes on the materials. The fact that Pakistan does not get along well with the neighboring country of India, which is also a nuclear power, gives the United States good reason to be concerned about the instability and strife in this part of the world.

Faith & Fear

That which theology has clearly taught, history must teach to those who choose to learn by experience, if indeed they will listen. Humanity refuses to look into the mirror and see its darker, more dangerous side. God's judgment of humanity's condition just prior to the great flood is blunt: "The LORD saw that the wickedness of man was great on the earth, and that every intent of the thoughts of his heart was only evil continually" (Genesis 6:5-6). It wasn't God who turned stones into weapons, wood into bows, and iron into swords. Nor did he lead man to split the atom for destructive purposes. And it will not be God who transforms medical equipment used for healing into a radiological disaster. These weapons of harm and destruction are human inventions, and God did not design for people to be at enmity with one another.

It is remarkable that people in the twenty-first century still find it difficult to believe that human beings would want to annihilate one another. Human history is a story of wars and unstable peace between wars. It is a story of peoples looking for love and peace, in ways that seem right to them, in every place but heaven. King David wrote, "The fool has said in his heart, 'There is no God.' They are corrupt, they have committed abominable deeds; there is no one who does good. The LORD has looked down from heaven upon the sons of men to see if there are any who understand, who seek after God. They have all turned aside, together they have become corrupt; there is none who does good, not even one" (Psalm 14:1-3). Without God, the true God, humanity—in the name of "whatever" or "whoever"—will always do what it does best: destroy peace with *whatever weapon is available.*

10

Targeting Terrorism Justly

A Biblical Perspective
on War and Terrorism

Freedom and fear, justice and cruelty, have always been at war, and we know that God is not neutral between them.

President George W. Bush
September 20, 2001

The Bible is very clear that love is to be the mark of the Christian, and the greatest good that a believer can do is to practice Christian love in every area of life. The greatest good that a society or nation can practice is that of justice for the citizens of that nation. Personal ethics and corporate ethics are two different sides of one coin—each has distinctive features.

In his address before Congress and the American people on September 20, 2001, President Bush said of the war on terrorism, "Whether we bring our enemies to justice, or justice to our enemies, justice will be done." With these words he voiced a moral, ethical, and biblical response in the present war against

155

terrorism. And it is a response that is built upon a centuries-old Christian view of warfare known as "just war theory." Just war theory offers Christians guiding principles for when to go to war and how to conduct war. What exactly are these principles?

"Kill 'em all, and let God sort 'em out!" That is one of many statements that were expressed by Americans after the 9/11 attacks. And it is a phrase that is commonly heard in discussions about war and terrorism. But, is such a viewpoint appropriate? Is it ethical and, more importantly, is it biblical? What are we to make of this slogan that is occasionally expressed in civilian and military environments—sometimes jokingly, sometimes seriously? Is it humorous or repulsive? Is it biblical or blasphemous? Interestingly, though it is cropping up everywhere today in conversations, on bumper stickers, on T-shirts, it is not a new sentiment. In fact, it expresses the feelings of a "Christian" religious leader nearly a 1,000 years ago who, when asked by a military commander on the battlefield for assistance in distinguishing between Christians and non-Christians, replied, "Kill them all. God will know which are his." The latter half of the response may be theologically correct—God does know—but the first half is morally repugnant. It was, however, fully accepted and acted upon as a "Christian response." That's a clear illustration of the fact that values have consequences. This leader's did, and so do ours. What, then, is a proper view of how to fight terrorism and wage a war?

Terrorism, War, and Sin

In addressing the biblical response to terrorism, we must first place terrorism in the context of war, sin, and evil. Terrorism is one part of the larger concept of warfare. Thus, if we first have a response to the broader issue of war, we can then apply that response to one specific part—terrorism.

If we truly believe that our faith matters and that the Bible should be applied to every area of our lives, then we must think about its application in global affairs as well as family, church, vocational, and community life. When a Christian begins to think about how to apply his or her faith to the realm of warfare, these are some of the first questions that must be addressed: What should be the Christian's attitude and response to the deaths and devastation caused by war? Is war moral, immoral, or amoral? Are all wars the same morally and ethically? When can Christians participate in war? When should Christians abstain from participation in or protest against a war? Can Christians fight against other Christians? If we end up having to go to war, does Christianity provide any guidance for the conduct of war, on either a strategic or personal level? What is there in Christian doctrine that promotes war, and what is there in Christian doctrine that promotes peace? Throughout Christianity's 2,000-year history, Christians have justified, rationalized, restrained, and informed the act of war and the conduct of warfare. They have, in various times and by various means, both upheld and departed from biblical standards, and both ecclesiastical and secular leaders have appealed to Christianity's teachings for personal and national guidance and support.

Whenever there is war, there are four elements that come together to determine the course of the conflict: government, the military, the public, and technology. Behind these four elements of war there are many influences. Religious values are only one factor, yet religion in general—and Christianity specifically—has been a major factor in the history of warfare. There has not, however, been unanimity in the Christian response to war. While, as we will see, there has been a prevailing Christian perspective or Christian doctrine of war, there have been several Christian positions articulated on war. Each of these viewpoints has its own history, and each has claimed biblical authority and support.

The apostle Paul wrote, "If possible, so far as it depends on you, be at peace with all men" (Romans 12:18). Yet history and news headlines provide ample proof that peace cannot always be the Christian response to the evil that people and nations perpetrate. Before we can think theologically about the *conduct* of war—and our conduct in war—we must think theologically about the *cause* of war. In short, we must consider war and the problem of evil.

At the foundation of the Christian understanding of war is a belief in the fallen and broken nature of humanity. The Bible teaches that all of humanity and every aspect of personal and corporate life are marred by sin and original sin. Our sin nature corrupts international relations as well as interpersonal relations. War is ultimately a reflection of and a consequence of sin. The Russian author Aleksandr Solzhenitsyn, who was both a soldier and a political prisoner under the Stalin regime, said of the widespread effects of sin that "gradually it was discerned to me that the line separating good and evil passes not through states, nor between classes, nor between political parties either—but right through every human heart."[1]

Wars are fought on the battlefields of the globe, but they are waged first in human hearts. It is in this light that Christian philosopher Arthur Holmes wrote, "To call war anything less than evil would be self-deception. The Christian conscience has throughout history recognized the tragic character of war. The issue that tears the Christian conscience is not whether war is good, but whether it is in all cases avoidable."[2] The death, destruction, horror, and personal and property losses of war are real issues. For a Christian to think about and wrestle with the issues of war is to struggle with the problem of evil.

The Christian Spectrum of War

Christians throughout history have recognized that the formulation of a doctrine of war or approach to war is a theological and biblical deduction based upon the interpretation of numerous passages in the Bible (cf. Ecclesiastes 3:1,8; Matthew 5:44; 24:6-7; Acts 10:1-23; Romans 13:1-7; 1 Timothy 2:2; 1 Peter 2:13-17). How those passages are interpreted determines the position that one holds. There is no "red letter" version of the Bible on the doctrine of war. Thus the issue is not "What is the Bible's view of war?" but "What view best interprets and reflects the biblical passages regarding war?"

The Christian response to war has ranged from absolute rejection of war and participation in it to full participation with the proclamation of divine blessing and authority. The spectrum has ranged from the pacifist words of the American folk hymn, "Gonna lay down my sword and shield down by the riverside, ain't gonna study war no more" to the cry of the Crusaders of the Middle Ages, "God wills it!" More specifically, the spectrum of Christian participation in war runs as follows: pacifism, nonresistance, just war, preventive war, and crusade. For each of these views there are secular as well as religious counterparts—that is, pacifism and Christian pacifism, just war and Christian just war, and so on. Each view also has strengths and weaknesses and variations. At the two ends of the spectrum are pacifism and the crusade, and the "just war" position is the moderating position and is the view that has been most prevalent throughout church history. It is also a view that was developed largely by Christians (especially Ambrose, Augustine, and Thomas Aquinas).

Critics of pacifism note that the principal problem with pacifism is that it misidentifies the morality of the individual as justification for (or morality of) the behavior of the state. At the other end of the spectrum, the principal problem with the crusade is that the church incorrectly identifies itself with the function of the state—specifically, a theocratic state. The church wrongly usurps the function of the state. With those facts in mind, let's take a closer look at the just war position.

Just a War or Just War?

The just war tradition has developed over a period of hundreds of years. It was heavily influenced by Christianity, but it also drew from Roman law and Greek philosophy. A list of just war criteria has emerged over the centuries—criteria for judging the appropriateness of going to war and to govern the conduct of military forces in war. Before looking at the criteria, it is worth noting the presuppositions of just war theory, of which there are four: [3]

1. The just war position recognizes that some evil cannot be avoided. In our actions and moral decisions in life, we strive for a biblical perspective. We strive to apply black and white to a world of gray, and sometimes "we are trapped in moral dilemmas whose roots lie in the past as well as the present, such that whatever we do involves us in evil of some sort."[4] We can never underestimate the ramifications of sin.

2. The just war position is normative for all people, both Christian and non-Christian. It doesn't describe how people do act, but how they should act, and it applies to all people.

3. The just war position does not try to justify war. Rather, it attempts to bring war within the limits of justice so that if everyone were guided by these principles, many wars would be eliminated.

4. The just war position assumes that individuals or private citizens do not have the right to use military force. Only governments have such a right. Thus, the key issue is not whether an individual can fight in war, but whether a government has the right to engage in armed conflict, and whether a citizen, Christian or not, should participate as an agent of that government.

Having said that, what, then, are the criteria for war? There are two categories, known as *jus ad bellum* (literally, "on the way to war"), in which the criteria determine *when resorting to war is justifiable* or *when to go to war*, and *jus in bello* (literally, "in the midst of war"), in which the criteria dictate *how war is to be justly conducted.* What are these criteria, which we can use as a checklist?

Principles of War

Within the two categories of criteria for war, there are seven principles or criteria for the just war. The first five principles apply as a nation is "on the way to war" *(jus ad bellum)*, and the final two apply to military forces "in the midst of war" *(jus in bello)*. Briefly, they are as follows:

1. Just cause—All aggression is condemned in just war theory. Participation in a war must be prompted by a just cause or defensive cause. No war of unprovoked aggression can ever be justified. Only defensive war is legitimate.

2. Just intention (right intention)—War must have a just intention; that is, its intent must be to secure a fair peace for all parties involved. Therefore, revenge, conquest, economic gain, and ideological supremacy are not legitimate motives for going to war. There must be a belief that, ultimately, greater good than harm will result from the war.

3. Last resort—War must be engaged in only as a last resort. Other means of resolution such as diplomacy and economic pressure must have been exhausted.

4. Formal declaration—War must be initiated with a formal declaration by properly constituted authorities. Only governments can declare war, not individuals, terrorist organizations, mercenaries, or militias.

5. Limited objectives—War must be characterized by limited objectives. This means that securing peace is

the goal and purpose of going to war. War must be waged in such a way that once peace is attainable, hostilities cease. Complete destruction of a nation's political institutions or economic institutions is an improper objective.

6. Proportionate means—Combatant forces of the opposition may not be subjected to greater harm than is necessary to secure victory and peace. The types of weapons and amount of force used must be limited to what is needed to repel aggression, deter future attacks, and secure a just peace. Therefore, total or unlimited warfare is inappropriate.

7. Noncombatant immunity—Military forces must respect individuals and groups not participating in the conflict and must abstain from attacking them. Since only governments can declare war, only governmental forces or agents are legitimate targets. This means that prisoners of war, civilians, and casualties are immune from intentional attacks.

The interpretation and application of these seven rules is not easy in modern warfare. Nor is there any assurance that they will always receive strict adherence. Warfare is not clean or nice; it is horrible. These principles are used not to promulgate war, but to contain it. They are principles of containment, not principles of conflagration. They are moral and ethical guidelines intended to help minimize the death and devastation that always accompany war.

So What?

Just war theory has three important functions. First, it seeks to limit the outbreak and devastation of war. Second, it offers a common moral framework and language for discussing issues of war in the public arena. As Christians and as citizens, it gives us a starting point for discussion and cultural engagement. And third, just war theory gives moral guidance to individuals in developing their conscience, responsibilities, and response. When the war drums sound, they are often loud, and there is frequently confusion, competition, and chaos rather than clear thinking about the moral and biblical consequences of what is occurring. Just war theory is a tool for responsible Christian living and citizenship.

War is a multifaceted event with multiple causes. Often what keeps a war going is different from what started it. Once wars begin, they follow a unique course all their own. From one perspective, war is "open armed conflict about power or territory involving centrally organized fighters and fighting with continuity between clashes."[5] Yet the definition and the experience of war are two vastly different things. At the beginning of the twentieth century, most casualties of war were military (85–90 percent). But in World War II, more than half of all war deaths involved noncombatants. And in the first half of the 1990s, 70 international states were involved in 93 wars, which killed five-and-a-half million people.[6] Most of those casualties were civilians, or noncombatants. At the end of the twentieth century, more than three-fourths of all war deaths were comprised of civilians.[7]

Just war is a Christian response to the tragedy of war, but it must be understood and applied by all who seriously believe that the Bible speaks with authority today. There *is* a time for war. C. S. Lewis, a veteran of World War I, wrote, "If war is ever lawful, then peace is sometimes sinful."[8] Issues of war and peace are very serious and have enormous personal, ethical, social, and theological ramifications. What you believe is important, for it affects how you live. The apostle Paul encouraged us to pray "for kings and all who are in authority, so that we may lead a tranquil and quiet life in all godliness and dignity" (1 Timothy 2:2). His words speak directly to the issues of warfare, spirituality, and evangelism. As you read the headlines, watch the news, and consider war, do so from a biblical perspective. Christian responsibility is not an option for the disciple of Jesus Christ, and this is especially true as we now consider a new kind of war—a war on terrorism.

Terrorism—Thinking It Through Theologically

A response to terrorism can be developed through the moral, ethical, and biblical model of just war theory. This is an area of just war theory that has not been addressed much in the past because terrorism had not yet reached the global proportions that it has reached today.

Terrorism is an asymmetric type of war. Those who practice it do so in part because they do not have the weapons or forces to engage nations in open combat on land or sea. That, however, does not make their actions justifiable. Terrorism expert Christopher C. Harmon observes:

> Terrorism is violence which no moral person can like, or ethically approve. The essence of terrorism includes immoral kinds of calculations: singling out victims who are innocent; and bloodying that innocence to shock and move a wider audience. To this doubly immoral path of political action, terrorists sometimes add the deliberate use of weapons that are nonselective in their killing range. By attacking citizens in peacetime with such indiscriminate means as car bombs and grenades, terrorists become the moral equivalent of war criminals in time of war....The terrorist admits of no contradiction between speaking warmly of "the people" but also fighting "for them" with bombs of compressed gas and nails that kill and burn passers-by. Such acts are abhorrent to nearly any civilization or any time and place. Indeed, one could well argue that if terrorism is not immoral, then nothing is immoral.[9]

Yet, regardless of what the terrorist does, our responses to terrorist acts should remain within the just war framework. For example, terrorists may not adhere to the ethical principles of discrimination and proportionality, but those who fight terrorism must do so. Shortly after the bombing of the U.S. embassies in Kenya and Tanzania by operatives of Osama bin Laden and the al-Qaeda terrorist network, James Turner Johnson, a philosopher and ethicist, wrote, "The reference point for thinking morally about responses to terrorism should be the just war tradition."[10]

Terrorism has no place in the world of ethical responses to the necessity of war. It is never morally permissible. In fact, it is the very opposite—it is morally reprehensible. Christopher C. Harmon states it well:

> Terrorism presents moral challenges because it is a kind of political depravity. One might say that if terrorism is not wrong, then nothing in politics or war can be condemned and all should be permitted.
>
> The use of terrorism is no indication of the justice of the avowed cause. The choice of terrorism may or may not be made out of desperation but it is, quite simply, an evil choice."[11]

In using the just war framework, what concerns or new questions must be asked in the war against terrorism? As Johnson states, "Moral reflection is not doing its job when it is employed only in retrospect, in response to particular terrorist acts."[12]

In an extended remark, Johnson notes some of the issues with which we must wrestle in a real world of war and terror:

> Is the good accomplished proportional to the means used? Are there any other means of dealing with the problem that have a reasonable hope of success? Both historically and logically, these concerns are secondary to those termed "necessary"; yet they are nonetheless important additional guidelines for moral policy and decisions regarding potential uses of force. In particular, these prudential criteria remind us that the use of military force is neither the preferred nor the only

option for dealing with terrorism. As awesome a
weapon as the cruise missile is, for example, its availability does not diminish the importance of other
weapons in the struggle against terrorism: policies
aimed at cutting off terrorist capabilities, removing
their support, eliminating conditions in which they tend
to flourish, gathering and sharing intelligence about
individual terrorists and terrorist organizations, and
bringing them to justice. A moral policy on dealing
with terrorism should incorporate such approaches
along with the possibility of resort to moral force.[13]

Issues such as those above as well as others like civilian
casualties, positive identification of terrorists, and targeting terrorists who often hide equipment and people in places like
schools, houses of worship, and hospitals are some of the many
problems and dilemmas that must be addressed repeatedly as
military operations and other efforts against terrorists continue.
Questions regarding the limits of a just war against terrorism
must be asked, as well as questions regarding the termination
of that war and issues related to the posthostility environment.

Augustine, one of the early and seminal thinkers on the
matter of Christianity and just war, stated that the greatest
danger in war is not the physical harm that it causes, but rather,
the passions that it inspires. That is a serious reminder to all
who enter armed conflict in any form. As the struggle against
terrorism continues and changes, we must also remember the
dictum of the great Prussian military theorist Carl von Clausewitz that war is never final.[14] If Clausewitz is right, the memory
of past conflict, motivation for future conflict, and methods for
a new type of conflict are almost certain.

We must not allow ourselves to be duped into the miscon-
ception that "one man's terrorist is another man's freedom
fighter." Such statements are built upon an ethical relativism
that rejects objective and absolute truth. Terrorism is morally,
ethically, and biblically indefensible. And regardless of one's

religious perspective, terrorism is an abuse of human rights and morally affects all people, whether or not they are personally targeted, injured, or killed.[15]

The present struggle and war against terrorism is one that will likely go on for a long time and be global in its reach. That does not make it unjust. But there are many questions to be answered in the course of this fight against terrorism. Those questions and their answers can guide us as we try to deal ethically and biblically with terrorism. The war can be won, but the victory must be moral as well as military.

Faith & Fear

The effects of the fall of Adam and Eve in the Garden of Eden have touched us all. Sin and the sin nature permeate all of life, and we must be biblical and realistic in our worldview and daily living. War is tragic, and the effects are real and lasting. No nation or Christian should ever enter into the realm of war without a profound sense of regret. But interestingly, war is not the greatest evil humans experience.

In 1939, with the storm clouds of war beginning their sweep across Europe in what would soon become a global war, C. S. Lewis was asked to speak to students at Oxford about the crisis of their day. He did so, encouraging them to maintain a Christian worldview and biblical perspective on life and death, war and peace, and the living of each day. He reminded them, "The war creates no absolutely new situation: it simply aggravates the permanent human situation so that we can no longer ignore it. Human life has always been lived on the edge of a precipice. Human culture has always had to exist under the shadow of something infinitely more important than itself....We are mistaken when we compare war with 'normal life.' Life has never been normal."[16]

Certainly those words are applicable to us today. Christians are called to carry out their service to God and others each and every day, regardless of the trials and tragedies that come our way. With God's grace and guidance, we can do so in the midst of life and death, tranquility and terror, peace and war.

11

Truth in Turbulent Times
Clear Thinking on Critical Issues

We—all of us, but especially the young—need around us individuals who possess a certain nobility, a largeness of soul, and qualities of human excellence worth imitating and striving for.[1]

William J. Bennett
Former Secretary of Education

Man's character is ultimately defined by the character of his god.[2]

Carl F. H. Henry
Theologian

America is a great country with a heritage rooted firmly in biblical values. Our love for our nation is enormous, and many of us pray for its continuation and a return to standards that reflect its Christian heritage. But we are not God's chosen people, and our Constitution remains subject to the philosophies and interests of its most recent interpreters. As President Franklin D. Roosevelt expressed, America is a nation

169

that works to protect freedom of speech, freedom to worship the god of one's choosing, freedom from want, and freedom from fear. As long as its citizens' pursuit of life, liberty, and happiness is generally fashioned by a moral standard consistent with God's character, it may endure. Yet the Christian's allegiance must first and foremost be to God. Regardless of the fate of our nation or any other nation, we must maintain a biblical perspective on past and current events.

Where you stand determines what you see. That is true physically, politically, and philosophically. The images of September 11, 2001 were very vivid and will remain with us for a long time. Our perspectives about the day's events, meaning, and significance are also important, and they are determined by our worldview. That worldview reflects who we are as individuals, as Americans, and as Christians.

Freedom is a wonderful thing when the beliefs we hold and the actions we take as citizens are consistent with the standards of justice and righteousness found in the Bible. However, freedom for the sake of freedom is a shrouded sword that, in time, will sever the moral tenets of society from God's standards if it is not grounded in the teachings of the Bible. Without biblical truth, men and women can end up projecting their own attitudes and aspirations as the mind of God, and God can end up becoming a physical or metaphysical idol. Ultimately, there are only two religions in the world: the religion of people in its many forms, and the religion of God. Either we worship the true God of the Bible, or we worship false gods of our own creation. If we choose the latter, we will suffer spiritual starvation, and "truth-famine is the ultimate and worst of all famines."[3] We must therefore choose wisely, for our choice will determine not only how we view life, but also, how we live life.

"Where was God?"

When trials and tragedies occur, a common question people ask is, "If there is a God, how could he allow such a horrible thing?" It is not a new question, yet with this question and similar ones, the person and character of God are challenged. The One who is the very essence of good and has no sin is challenged by those who have a sin nature and whose very essence is evil. The problem of evil is very real, but God is not the cause of evil in the world. Rather, evil is found in humanity, which has turned away from God and gone its own way. God did not create the world and then leave it to fate. He gave it to men and women as a stewardship, and we took it and went in every way but the way God wanted (Isaiah 53:6a).

If God had not pursued us, humanity would have no salvation or hope (Isaiah 53:6b,11) and the human race would have perished centuries ago. Only because of God's grace did Noah's family survive the great flood, the first global cataclysm. The psalmist writes:

> Good and upright is the LORD; therefore He instructs sinners in the way. He leads the humble in justice, and He teaches the humble His way. All the paths of the LORD are lovingkindness and truth to those who keep His covenant and His testimonies. For your name's sake, O LORD, pardon my iniquity, for it is great (Psalm 25:8-11).

Note that "all the paths of the LORD" lead to good, and that which permits us to enter this path is humility and the acceptance of his authority in our lives. This is a message for all people and a call to a personal relationship with God. Where God is misrepresented, ignored, or rejected, good is doused. And where good is doused, evil abounds.

Though most of the suffering we endure as human beings is the natural consequence of life lived in a fallen and imperfect world, some incidents, such as the mass killings by terrorists in the attacks of 9/11, point to something more sinister. They are examples of the extent to which a person will go whose mind and heart are far from God. As long as people devise their own visions of God, those views which are the most radical will be evidenced by the most extreme measures. People who hold radical views will inevitably express themselves in radical ways. Until the Lord returns, the rain—and the hail—will continue to fall on the just and the unjust alike. The way in which we respond to the hail reflects the depth or the shallowness of our faith and therefore determines the effectiveness of our Christian witness.

Some tragedies may be judgments of God or the result of His decision not to involve himself proactively. When people ask, "Where is God in the midst of tragedy?" a biblical response may sometimes be "watching," "waiting," or "working." We should not be surprised if God removes his providential hand from places in society where he is not welcome. Choices are free in America, but the consequences of those choices may be very costly. Americans must choose wisely. But we must also remember that there are many things we do not know about God's working. Christian ethicist and theologian Dennis P. Hollinger writes of what can and cannot be known of God's actions with regard to evil:

> In the aftermath of September 11, many have yearned for certainty regarding God's actions on that day. Where was God and what was God up to? It's only natural to seek certainty in the divine realm, for it brings consolation in the face of threat and evil in our world....But clearly, there are some things about divine actions we just do not know, and this is especially true of the ways of God in human history—his judgments, action and permissions in the world. As Isaiah the prophet put it, "For as the heavens are higher than the earth, so are my ways and my thoughts than your thoughts" (55:9).[4]

Often, where we want certainty we instead face silence, and we must not be guilty of assigning divine motives for human tragedies.

If the destruction of 9/11 is a judgment, as some have suggested, then the lack of an appropriate response by society and the church in America may prevent a successful effort to defeat terrorism. However, it is equally possible that the events of 9/11 are a wake-up call to force us to deal with an evil that has been growing in the world for more than 30 years. "It is quite clear that God's judgment comes in history; it is less clear how it comes. For one thing, the judgment of God is always at work against human sin and injustice, as there are continual reverberations from actions and character that fly in the face of God."[5]

Until recently, faith-based terrorists and their supporters have not been taken seriously by many nations in the world. Radical views have silenced the gospel in many places around the world, such as Sudan and Indonesia.[6] Secular America, with all of its social and moral weakness, has not done what the Taliban regime did to the people in Afghanistan. It is time to end terrorism's murderous rampage and for Islamic and other countries to have enough confidence in the merits of the religions they profess that they willingly allow their people the opportunity to choose any faith they desire.

God is in the world and always standing within reach of rebellious men and women, waiting and longing for them to turn and come into his open arms. He will not force himself on anyone. He is as near or as far away as people want him to be, but he is always present, good, and just.

God is as faithful on one day as he is on another, and, even in the presence of evil, God's work of redemption continues. In our sorrow over an evil act, we may see only darkness and be blind to the good that is everywhere to be seen. There is meaning and purpose in life, even in sorrow, and there is hope because God exists and is in constant pursuit of humanity. "And so, as we seek to understand God's presence and ways on September 11, 2001, we may see mystery, not certitude. But, in that mystery we find the hope of the world that binds our wounds, evokes our trust, ensures our freedom, and guides our paths for a journey in a very precarious world."[7]

Though we are served well by science and technology, in the end, and in the turbulent times, these will not save us. Our help and hope comes from God through eternal salvation and moral guidance. Thus the psalmist said:

> I will lift up my eyes to the mountains; from whence shall my help come? My help comes from the LORD, who made heaven and earth. He will not allow your foot to slip; He who keeps you will not slumber. Behold, He who keeps Israel will neither slumber nor sleep. The LORD is your keeper; the LORD is your shade on your right hand. The sun will not smite you by day, nor the moon by night. The LORD will protect you from all evil; *He will keep your soul*" (Psalm 121:1-7, emphasis added).

Ultimately, it is the soul and not the body that is most in the need of protection.

All You Need Is Love...Or Is It?

After the attacks of 9/11, some religious and secular voices claimed that love was all that was needed for there to be peace. As terrorists declared war, there were some who said our response should be forgiveness—but it was a forgiveness that ignored justice. Scripture states that God loves the whole world and does not wish anyone to perish (2 Peter 3:9), but his love for the world has mostly been rejected and, therefore, his relationship with most of the world is still broken because no forgiveness for sin has been accepted. And what is the consequence when love is rejected? Conflict, both great and small, in interpersonal and international relations. In a perfect world, love is all that a society needs. But in a fallen world, love alone may not be enough to secure peace.

Some people have too narrow a view of love, while others have too broad a view. Both extremes are unbiblical. Love is variously promoted as the way to suppress an enemy, the absence of pain, the only source of happiness, the only path to friendship, that which makes everything just the way you want it, a good feeling, or even an unattainable dream. The following quotes reflect such descriptions of love, and the italicized words identify the narrowness of each statement:

- "*Always love* your enemies—nothing annoys them so much" (Oscar Wilde).

- "One word *frees us of all* the weight and pain in life. That word is love" (Sophocles).

- "There is *only one happiness* in life, to love and to be loved" (George Sand).

- "Love is the *only force capable* of transforming an enemy into a friend" (Martin Luther King, Jr.).

- "The sound of a kiss is not so loud as the sound of a cannon, but *its echo lasts a great deal longer*" (Oliver Wendell Holmes).

- "The world is too dangerous for anything but truth, and *too small for anything but love*" (William Slone Coffin).

- "Put away the book, the description, the tradition, the authority, and take the journey of self-discovery. Love, and don't be caught in opinions and ideas about what love is or should be. *When you love, everything will come right.* Love has its own action. Love, and you will know the blessing of it. Keep away from the authority that tells you what love is or what it is not. No authority knows and he who knows cannot tell. Love, and there is understanding" (Krishnamurti).[8]

Such half-truths are always dangerous and deceptive. If there were no evil in the world, the statements might be more valid. But love doesn't exist alone or in a vacuum. In fact, it has little meaning apart from obedience to God. Without recognition of a divine authority and standard, love becomes whatever one wants it to be. Adam and Eve were the first people to demonstrate self-love when they disobeyed God. God had said to them: "From any tree of the garden you may eat freely; but from the tree of the knowledge of good and evil you shall not eat, for in the day that you eat from it you will surely die" (Genesis 2:16b-17). But they ate the forbidden fruit, and in so doing demonstrated their love of self more than of God. To defy God is to love self more than God. This is the first perversion of love. It is impossible to genuinely love when our actions exclude or ignore the known will of God. A person's understanding of love narrows or is weakened as he or she moves away from God.

Without obedience to God, love is always skewed, as is every other character trait. A failing in these other qualities compounds the distortion of love. Love without truth sends the wrong message; love without justice harms your neighbor; love without accountability destroys peace; love that tolerates evil deeds is an accomplice in these deeds. Love is hypocritical unless it abhors evil and seeks to do what is good and right (see Romans 12:9).

Jesus' appeal in Matthew 5:44 for Christians to love and pray for their enemies was stated in opposition to the Pharisees' narrow view of love: love your friends and hate your enemies. Christians are to live at peace with all people as much as is possible (Romans 12:18), but sometimes it is not possible. One of Christianity's remarkable features is its call for Christians to love in the extreme, even to the point of suffering, if suffering will help to open the eyes of those who disbelieve. To hate without having first sought to love contradicts the intention and character of God.

The primary responsibility of each Christian is to reflect the love of God for humanity in every situation. But Christians have another responsibility that is often neglected: to reflect the love of God, they must also reflect God's holiness—that is, righteousness and justice. Holiness entails his hatred of evil and of those who persist in committing it.[9]

God Loves the Sinner but Hates the Sin?

Is it wrong to hate Osama bin Laden? Even in turbulent times, many would say that hating bin Laden would be sinful. But like love, the concept of hate also has been skewed and misunderstood, as is seen in the following examples that reflect an improper view of it:

- "Hate and mistrust are the *children of blindness*" (Sir William Watson).

- "If you hate a person, you hate something within him that is a part of yourself. *What isn't a part of ourselves doesn't disturb us*" (Herman Hesse).

- "*It is easy to hate* and it is difficult to love. This is how the whole scheme of things works. All good things are difficult to achieve; and *bad things are very easy to get*" (Morarji Desai).

- "Always remember others may hate you but *those who hate you don't win unless you hate them*. And then you destroy yourself" (Richard Nixon).

- "Hating people is *like burning down your own house* to get rid of a rat" (Henry Emerson Fosdick).

- "Perhaps no phenomenon contains so much destructive feeling as 'moral indignation,' which permits envy or *hate to be acted out under the guise of virtue*" (Erich Fromm).[10]

From a biblical perspective, none of these statements is true. Some may be true of hatred that is baseless, self-centered and ungodly, but there is a hatred that is holy and justified. There is no question that the hatred that we see so much of in the media, in movies, in unjust wars, and between ethnic, racial, and social groups is wrong. It is unjustified, destructive, and morally indefensible. But to combine all hatreds into one horrible heap is to lessen the value and meaning of love. A biblical hatred is one that protects others from evil. Hate is love's opposite only when it is selfish and baseless.

Sinners in the Hands of an Angry God—God's Hatred of Sinful Humanity

Evil is propagated by people whose hearts are rebellious and self-centered. Without the freedom of choice, sin's debilitating and destructive nature would have no foundation from which to work. Humanity's misunderstanding of hatred makes it difficult for many to believe that God can or does hate sinful people. But the scriptural evidence is very clear and supports the claim that "God is hostile to both the sinner and his sin. The deed is punished with the doer."[11] It is the understanding of God's immense hatred for sin and for those who choose its lifestyle that makes the mystery of the cross of Christ, and therefore his love, so much more meaningful and profound. God's hatred for human sinfulness is equaled by the intensity of his love for humanity. Through the work of Jesus Christ on the cross, the condemnation of humanity is abolished.

The following are scriptures that teach about God's hatred of evil deeds and evildoers:

- "For You are not a God who takes pleasure in wickedness; no evil dwells with You. The boastful shall not stand before Your eyes; You hate all who do iniquity. You destroy those who speak falsehood; the LORD abhors the man of bloodshed and deceit" (Psalm 5:4-6).

- "The LORD tests the righteous and the wicked, and the one who loves violence His soul hates" (Psalm 11:5).

- "There are six things which the LORD hates, yes, seven which are an abomination to Him: haughty eyes, a lying tongue, and hands that shed innocent blood, a heart that devises wicked plans, feet that run rapidly to evil, a false witness who utters lies, and one who spreads strife among brothers" (Proverbs 6:16-19).

- "All their evil is at Gilgal; indeed, I came to hate them there! Because of the wickedness of their deeds I will drive them out of My house! I will love them no more; all their princes are rebels" (Hosea 9:15; see also Jeremiah 12:8).

Biblical hatred is more of an attitude than an emotion. It is a strong aversion to and rejection of evil and of those who sponsor it, as evident in these words from the psalmist: "Your lovingkindness is before my eyes, and I have walked in Your truth. I do not sit with deceitful men, nor will I go with pretenders. I hate the assembly of evildoers, and I will not sit with the wicked, I shall wash my hands in innocence, and I will go about Your altar, O LORD" (Psalm 26:3-6; see also Psalm 139:19-24).

Biblical hatred is repulsed by, intolerant of, and opposed to everything that is evil and undermines good. It is an attitude that protects each Christian from sin's subtle intrusion into his or her life. Often, the things that threaten us most are those about which we are unaware or of which we are inappropriately tolerant. A wrong understanding or a toleration of evil guarantees that evil will creep ever closer until it corrupts what is good. Eventually, a continued toleration of evil causes the essence of evil to be viewed as something that is good (cf. Romans 1:18-32).

Biblical hatred does not turn people into violent radicals; it makes them better peacemakers. Loving acts must always be sought and preferred. God loves each and every person, but often the choices and actions of individuals push aside God's love or reject it, leaving God's hatred for sin and those who commit it to decide their eternal destiny (Matthew 23:33-39). When Jesus Christ was crucified, the sins of the world, of all people, were placed upon him. But that gift must be accepted or rejected. God does not want anyone to be eternally separated from him, but he lets individuals choose for themselves (2 Peter 3:9). Without the judgment of the cross, there can be no true love or peace for anyone. Also, as stated in chapter 10, war is the domain of the state, not the individual. A Christian may participate in a just war, but it is not individuals who declare war.

The hatred and destruction of evil is in fact a loving act to those who are freed from evil's tyranny. We must always remember to distinguish between personal social ethics and the actions of the state. They may or may not be the same and, therefore, for individual Christians, hatred has three restrictions: 1) we can never hate God, 2) we are prohibited from hating our brothers and sisters in Christ (Leviticus 19:17; Deuteronomy 19:10-13; 1 John 4:7-10, 20-21), and 3) we are prohibited from violence of any sort except in self-defense.

The feeling of hatred for evil is natural, especially in the aftermath of something like the events of 9/11, but our hatred must be righteous indignation and not unbridled anger, for only then will we respond appropriately and seek justice rather than revenge.[12] Only then will we fight a war that is just. America must continue to control hatred with its just war principles, such as those of discrimination and proportionality, as discussed in the previous chapter.

God in the Hands of Angry Sinners—Human Hatred of a Loving God

Frequently, people accuse God of hatred. God's character is attacked with statements such as, "I know many good Jews and Muslims and others who aren't Christian. How can a loving God not also permit sincere people of other faiths into his eternal kingdom?" To call God unloving is to place one's own perspective above God's. Some are using America's war on terrorism as a platform for espousing theological universalism or inclusivism. Exclusivism, which is faithfulness to God and Christian doctrine alone, does not equate to hate and violence. We must not focus on peace on earth at the expense of peace with God. For example, Thomas L. Friedman of *The New York Times* wrote:

> The future of the world may well be decided by how we fight this war. Can Islam, Christianity and Judaism know that God speaks Arabic on Fridays, Hebrew on Saturdays, and Latin on Sunday, and that he welcomes different human beings approaching him through their own history, out of their language and cultural heritage? Many Jews and Christians have already argued that the answer to that question is yes, and some have gone back to their sacred texts to reinterpret their traditions to embrace modernity and pluralism, and to create space for secularism and alternative faiths.[13]

These are difficult words to read because they are biblically wrong. Words such as these reflect the doctrines and desires of those who see God as nothing more than the creation of the human mind or who acknowledge God but ignore his justice. They reflect an improper understanding of God. God is not a social construction, an intellectual idol. God is very real and He loves the world and understands that evil is the element that separates the world from him. His plan to overcome this separation has but one option: because the penalty for sin is death, he must provide the perfect sacrifice so that all peoples of every language and ethnic background can have a path back to righteousness and therefore to himself. He offers himself in the person of Jesus Christ as the sacrificial Lamb of God. For the sins of humanity, the Father watched his Son be brutally beaten and slain by the same humanity that he wants to save. The only action each of us must take is to accept this sacrificial death on our behalf, and our salvation is secured. A person is not a Christian by birth; he or she is a Christian by choice and conviction.

But much of humanity rejects the Son of God in favor of their own means of salvation—which always involves some type of human work that allows humanity to save itself—and then dares to call God unloving, uncaring, and too narrow. It is humanity that has rejected God and wants to replace him with secularism and modernity and, thereby, lead people further away from biblical hope and truth. The hatred that destroys resides in the hearts of people, not God. God's hatred of sin is only satisfied through the cross of Jesus Christ, which makes life available to anyone who trusts in its merit. God's hatred of sin and the sinner put Christ on the cross so that *all* could have life. Some choose instead to create their own gods, but they will suffer the consequences of their idolatry when God judges them.

Faith & Fear

Peace is not achieved by allowing everyone to believe what they want, whether it is right or wrong, but rather through belief in the same thing. And until the Lord returns, the best that people of different beliefs—though with similar morals— can achieve is a delicate peace that requires a real tolerance of those differences and refrains from forcing specific religious or secular convictions upon anyone.

Christianity offers the only true answer to hatred in the world: love and devotion to God because of his love for us. Our abhorrence of evil makes us the most loving people in the world. Share the gospel, and be a good neighbor to all. It is God's truth alone that can enable us to persevere through the turbulent times that remain until the return of our Lord and Savior Jesus Christ.

12

Triumph over Tragedy
Certain Hope in Uncertain Times

After this unspeakable crime, will anything ever be the same?[1]

The Economist
September 15, 2001

More than 60 years ago, on Sunday morning, December 7, 1941, Americans were shocked when they heard that their nation was under attack at Pearl Harbor. In the years that followed, a world war was fought and won, but at a great price. And the world was never the same again. So, too, in the aftermath of Tuesday morning, September 11, 2001, is a new war being fought around the globe. And the world will never be the same. Around the world there is agreement that life will be different in many respects for Americans and many others. What has emerged in the months since the attacks is not fear, but resolve—a resolve that a tragedy of such magnitude in such a manner will not happen again. No one is naïve enough to think that this means conflicts will cease, war will no longer be waged, and swords will be turned into ploughshares. But there is

183

a conviction that justice will be done with respect to the events of 9/11 and that the threat of terrorism will be diminished.

The Death of an Era

The cover of the British magazine *The Economist* for September 15, 2001 said it all. There was a picture of the smoking skyline of New York City and the words "The day the world changed." The magazine was right. The world did change that day. The collapse of the twin towers of the World Trade Center was more than the fall of a magnificent architectural feat. It was the fall of an era. When the walls of the World Trade Center and portions of the Pentagon crumbled, so too did the era of postmodernism. Artists, authors, economists, historians, politicians, philosophers, and theologians have recognized that we are now at the end of one age and the beginning of a new age. While there may not be agreement about what that new era is going to look like, few doubt that it now exists. Christian social critic Gene Edward Veith writes:

> Postmodernists rejected the very possibility of objective truth, insisting that reality is only a construction of the culture or of a mind. But the planes that crashed into the buildings and into every American's consciousness were no mental constructions. Objective reality in all of its hard edges asserted itself.[2]

In postmodern thought, there was a rejection of any possibility of objective truth or morals. Morality was relative. Right and wrong varied according to cultures, individuals, or circumstances. Right was decided by whatever people chose to be right for them. But all of that changed on 9/11. "The terrorists certainly made a *choice,* and what they did was right *for them.* But somehow their cold-blooded murder of thousands of ordinary men, women, and children was seen as pure evil, something postmodernists had professed not to believe in."[3]

For postmodernists, all cultures were the same and equally valid. Yet when Western civilization came under attack, its attackers were viewed as something to be repulsed. For more than a decade, Western civilization as an academic subject in universities had been viewed as not worth studying or saving; but instantly that had changed and "it began to be seen as something worth defending. It became hard to consider the havens of Islamic terrorism, which teach hatred, oppression, and suicide bombing, as really being equal to the land of the free."[4]

In the aftermath of the terrorist attacks, the slogan "True for you, but not for me" no longer holds much appeal. There is now an opportunity for Christians to reassert the historic teachings of Christianity and the biblical worldview. If we are going to speak effectively to our age, we must understand it.[5] We have a message of hope, certainty, and triumph to offer to all who will listen. The opening for these opportunities may well come in discussions about a subject that was rarely spoken of in public and private in the days prior to 9/11: the subject of evil.

The New Four-Letter Word

The covers of weekly news magazines, hosts on television talk shows, and newspapers throughout the world are using a word that hasn't been seen or heard in contemporary culture for a long time—*evil*. An essay in *Time* magazine stated, "One of the consequences of 9/11 has been to revive, so to speak, the belief in evil."[6]

When we trade the truth of God for the lies of Satan—when we follow Adam and Eve on the course of sin from the Garden of Eden rather than following Jesus Christ on the course of righteousness from the cross—we ultimately bring ourselves, and others, to ruin. In his book *Mere Christianity,* C. S. Lewis wrote that "wickedness when you examine it, turns out to be the pursuit of some good in the wrong way....evil is a parasite, not an original thing."[7]

Discussions about the nature, source, and course of evil are important. But for today's society, a first step has been taken back to a biblical perspective by simply acknowledging the reality of evil. Christians now have the opportunity to proclaim afresh the gospel of Jesus Christ. As journalist Andree Seu writes, "Ours is a Spirit of boldness, not timidity, that compels us to speak something—not nothing—into a world that, since Sept. 11, 2001, still picks through the ashes of despondency and stumbles at noon as in the dark."[8] In this moment, we have a message to proclaim. It is a message of love, not evil, and it is the love of Jesus Christ.

A Broken Heart but Not a Crushed Spirit

Jesus told his disciples, "In this world you have tribulation, but take courage; I have overcome the world" (John 16:33). There are indeed storm clouds over us, and there are more on the horizon. Yet Christians are called to maintain an eternal perspective as well as a temporal one. A personal relationship with Jesus Christ will not make us immune to trauma and tragedy in life, but it will give us a perspective and hope that the rest of the world does not have.

Looking at terrorism in the twenty-first century, terrorist expert Brian Jenkins states for contemporary American society,

> Our most effective defense against terrorism will come not from surveillance, concrete barriers, metal detectors, or new laws, but from our own virtue, courage, continued dedication to our ideals of a free society, realism in our acceptance of risk, stoicism, intelligence and the skepticism that comes with it, the avoidance of extremism, and the humanity and sense of community too fleetingly expressed when we mourn our dead. It will come from true patriotism.[9]

For the Christian, living effectively in this new age means that there is the additional call to discipleship and bearing the witness of Jesus Christ to a traumatized world. Christians are called to courage in this world, but that courage is to be rooted in the person and work of Jesus Christ.

In the ancient world, courage was a valued virtue, but it was seen as rooted in the inner resources of the individual. Not so with Christian courage. Christian courage is found solely in Jesus Christ. Theologian Carl F. H. Henry notes that the Christian view is distinct and rejects the classical perspective of virtue and courage based on self-strength alone:

> Christianity repudiates that speculation. Jesus anchors courage in His victory over the world achieved by His resurrection as the crucified One, a decisive historical event that sets Christian realities apart from pagan mythology. Not self-reliance, but Christ the Overcomer is the hinge of history. Our lives and mission are in the nail-scarred hands of the Victor who vanquished the threatening postures of the world powers. Jesus says, "Take courage!" Christian courage centers in and around the Messiah who by His sinless life and bodily resurrection won and guarantees the victory over all the powers of evil and oppression and even of death.[10]

Christians have hope in this world because they have the certainty of eternal life. Current events can be viewed with an eternal perspective—a perspective that understands that God is at work in the world and that he uses events, good and bad, for his purposes. In addition, this perspective recognizes there will come a time of divine reckoning and justice for all people. In that day, there will be eternal comfort and peace for those who are Christians, and it will be Jesus Christ who comforts us: "He will wipe away every tear from their eyes; and there will no longer be any death; there will no longer be any mourning, or crying, or pain; the first things have passed away" (Revelation 21:4). One day there will be a world without sorrow and terror.

A New Attitude, A New Perspective

As a nation and as individuals, we often forget our history and lose our perspective. We feel hopeless, unappreciated, and unwelcome. Sometimes we forget that the world doesn't end until God says so. How we feel about the condition of the world has no influence on his plans. God is the hand in the glove of history, and he permits peoples, nations, and empires to rise and fall according to his purposes and his plan for the ages.

Too often we forget history. We forget how sinful the world was before the flood. We forget how corrupt the nation of Israel became from the reign of Jeroboam until the nation's destruction in 722 B.C. We forget the moral decadence of Rome and the failure of the church during much of its history in the West. Some would even have us forget or rewrite the evils of Hitler and Nazi Germany and the brutalities of the Soviet Union under Stalin or the killing fields of Cambodia under the Khmer Rouge. Both the West and East have had more than enough dictators, tyrants, and oppressors.

Our nation has its shortcomings and failures, past and present, but it remains the greatest nation in the modern world. It is still a nation with great potential and a country where Christians have the freedom and opportunity to influence its future. Since 9/11, an opportunity to see it grow stronger and better has been opened to us—if we choose to take advantage of it.

Remember Abraham's concern for the righteous people who lived in two of the most wicked cities in biblical history, Sodom and Gomorrah. As he walked with God, it became clear to him that the destruction of these decadent cities was imminent. Immediately he focused on the righteous remnant that lived among the inhabitants of the first city upon which judgment would come. And he asked God, "Suppose there are fifty righteous within the city; will You indeed sweep it away and not spare the place for the sake of the fifty righteous who are in it?" (Genesis 18:24). Abraham was greatly concerned about justice and that the righteous and the wicked not be treated alike. God responded to Abraham by promising that he would indeed spare the city if he found 50 righteous people living among the wicked.

Abraham continued to decrease the number until he asked the Lord if he would spare the city for the sake of ten righteous inhabitants. Again, God said that he would do so. As long as one righteous person lived in Sodom, the city would not be judged. It was not until Lot and his immediate family departed from the city that destruction fell upon Sodom.

We are at a strategic moment in the history of our nation and for the church of Jesus Christ. These are difficult times, but it is not the end of the world. We should not let doomsday threats and attitudes of despair cause us to disengage from the affairs of the day. As long as the righteous live among the wicked, the salt of eternal truth and the light that reflects off our kind words and good deeds must be present in every place that Christians live. Our message is one of hope, not despair. As citizens, let us help in the destruction of terrorism and the bringing of evil-doers to justice, and may peace and hope be our message. We should not love everything about the world system, but we must choose to love its inhabitants as long as God permits us to live among them. Not everyone will come to Christ, but Christians must be Christ to all.

In these days, Christians are called to be a people of faith, letting the light of salvation shine into the darkness of the world. Jesus Christ told his disciples, "I am the light of the world" (see John 8:12). That Light is more than adequate for the darkness of these days. And the Christian responsibility is enormous. As Mark Galli of *Christianity Today* writes:

> To shoulder this responsibility at this historical moment is both a burden and a gift for Christians. But we must step into this future with humility, recognizing that we cannot know God's will perfectly at every political turn; with patience, knowing that the fight for liberty is never won in a single generation; with sadness, realizing that on this side of the kingdom, justice is often impossible without some violence; and with a serenity that passes understanding, abiding in God's grace for the meaning and measure of our lives.[11]

For all its terror, 9/11 provides an opportunity to heal America's broken heart. People are looking for answers that they previously thought they already knew. Christians must therefore act upon their faith and clearly represent the principles and values that have shaped this country and have historically been the foundation of its greatness. Nothing is irreversible where God is present.

Faith & Fear

We encourage you in these days to be knowledgeable of Scripture, confident in its truth, and always living out your faith before your neighbors, friends, family, and coworkers. Regardless of their religious affiliation, philosophical perspective, or ethnic background, share with them the love of Jesus Christ. We must present the truth and leave the results to God. Jesus told his disciples, "Let your light shine before men in such a way that they may see your good works, and glorify your Father who is in heaven" (Matthew 5:16). Christians are the reflection of a clear and certain hope in uncertain times that have a clear and present danger. It is because of our hope that we can have triumph over any and every tragedy.

Today and in the days ahead, let us remember that Christians have always lived in tenuous times. In the uncertainty of his days, and in circumstances that eventually led to his death, the apostle Paul wrote this exhortation to Titus and, now to us:

> The grace of God has appeared, bringing salvation to all men, instructing us to deny ungodliness and worldly desires and to live sensibly, righteously and godly in the present age, looking for the blessed hope and the appearing of the glory of our great God and Savior, Christ Jesus, who gave Himself for us to redeem us from every lawless deed, and to purify for Himself a people for His own possession, zealous for good deeds. These things speak and exhort and reprove with all authority. Let no one disregard you (Titus 2:11-15).

No Fear Through the Valley of the Shadow of Death

The subject of this volume is a very serious one, and throughout it we have discussed the issues of faith and fear in light of terrorism. In the aftermath of what took place on September 11, 2001, individuals and nations around the globe have been called upon to make a decision as to where they stand in relation to terrorism. They are being asked to act decisively and intentionally, and to demonstrate their allegiance to justice and peace. The response that is made will have enormous consequences in the future with regard to the issues of freedom, democracy, justice, human rights, war, and peace. It is our hope and prayer that the responses made are in accordance with biblical principles, both for the sake of the world and the sake of the gospel of Jesus Christ (see 1 Timothy 2:1-2).

There is, however, another decision that every person must make in life. It too is one that has enormous consequences, not only in this life, but for all of eternity. This decision is one that

191

is made in response to the call of Jesus Christ to accept or reject the salvation that he freely offers to all people. It is a salvation based upon his death on the cross for the sins of every person. Salvation brings to those who accept it not only the certainty of eternal life, but also perspective and resources for the living of these days. It does not remove us from the difficulties and circumstances of daily living in a world marred by sin, but it does give us help for the present and hope for the future. We must still walk through the valley of the shadow of death, but we do so with the certainty that God is with us and that the Holy Spirit will guide us.

Perhaps you have reached these final pages and do not have that assurance or do not yet know what your eternal destiny will be or how to obtain it. If so, then this is the most important portion of this book, and we encourage you to carefully consider its contents. Near the end of the Gospel of John, the apostle John wrote, "These [things] have been written so that you may believe that Jesus is the Christ, the Son of God; and that believing you may have life in His name" (John 20:31). We want you to know for sure that you have eternal life through Jesus Christ, God's Son.

God has made a provision, at no expense to you but at great expense to him, for you to enter into a relationship with him that will give you eternal life. But you must recognize and acknowledge that you need forgiveness of sin. The Bible says that in the eyes of God we are all sinners: "All have sinned and fall short of the glory of God" (Romans 3:23). God is holy and thus cannot ignore the sin of any person. He must judge it. However, God, in His mercy, has provided a way by which sinful men and women can receive His forgiveness. This forgiveness was provided at a great cost by Jesus Christ when he came to earth 2,000 years ago, lived a perfect life, and died on a cross in our place to pay for our sin: "For the wages of sin is death, but the free gift of God is eternal life in Jesus Christ our Lord" (Romans 6:23). The Bible also says that "Christ died for our sins according to the Scriptures, and that He was buried, and that He was raised on the third day according to the Scriptures" (1 Corinthians 15:3-4).

In order to obtain this salvation and eternal life that Jesus Christ offers, we must individually trust that Christ's payment through his death on the cross is the only way that we can receive the forgiveness of our sins, the reestablishment of a relationship with God, and eternal life. "By grace you have been saved through faith; and that not of yourselves, it is the gift of God; not as a result of works, so that no one may boast" (Ephesians 2:8-9).

Do you recognize your sin before God? If you do, then come to Jesus Christ, asking for forgiveness and requesting eternal life. If you do not acknowledge your need for salvation, then you bypass this opportunity. Please don't.

If you want the salvation God offers through the work of Jesus Christ, we encourage you to express that desire through the following prayer:

> Dear Lord,
>
> I know that I have done wrong and fallen short of Your perfect ways. I realize that my sins have separated me from You and that I deserve Your judgment. I believe that You sent Your Son, Jesus Christ, to earth to die on the cross for my sins. I put my trust in Jesus Christ and what He did on the cross as payment for my sins. Please forgive me and give me eternal life. Amen.

If you just prayed this prayer in sincerity, you are now a child of God and have eternal life. We encourage you to develop this wonderful relationship by learning more about God through the study of the Bible. We further encourage you to find a church that teaches God's Word, encourages fellowship with other Christians, and promotes the spreading of God's message of forgiveness to others.

If you were a Christian before reading this book, we encourage you to continue to grow in your relationship with

Jesus Christ and the knowledge of the Bible. Study and apply God's Word to your life daily, and nurture a worldview that reflects biblical principles and a concern for all of God's creation, especially men and women who have yet to hear the gospel of Jesus Christ. And in this world of terror and terrorism, stand firm and, with the grace of God, fear not.

Notes

Chapter 1—Terror Takes Its Toll

1. John V. Parachini, "The World Trade Center Bombers" in *Toxic Terror: Assessing Terrorist Use of Chemical and Biological Weapons*, Jonathan B. Tucker, ed. (Cambridge, MA: MIT Press, 2000), p. 191.
2. Ibid., p. 188.
3. Bernard Lewis, "The Revolt of Islam," *The New Yorker*, November 19, 2001, p. 51.
4. Ibid., pp. 51-52.
5. Karen Armstrong, *Islam: A Short Story* (New York: Random House, Inc., 2000), pp. 6, 29, 133, 157-58. "Social justice was, therefore, the crucial virtue of Islam. Muslims were commanded as their first duty to build a community (*ummah*) characterized by *practical compassion* [emphasis added], in which there was a fair distribution of wealth. This was far more important than any doctrinal teaching about God" (p. 6). "Salvation did not mean redemption from sin, but the creation of a just society in which the individual could more easily make that existential surrender of his or her whole being that would bring fulfillment" (pp. 157-58). Islam is a spiritual and political struggle to create the perfect society through which redemption can be realized. History (A.D. 610 to the present) records that success in this redemptive effort has been extremely difficult.
6. Salman Rushdie, "Yes, This Is About Islam," *New York Times*, November 2, 2001.
7. Bruce Hoffman, "Terrorism Trends and Prospects," *Countering the New Terrorism*, Ian O. Lesser et al., eds. (Santa Monica, CA: RAND, 1999), pp. 10-17.
8. President Bush's Address to a Joint Session of Congress and the American People, September 20, 2001. The speech can be found on the Internet at http://www.georgebush.com.
9. Jack Kelly, "Trainees Eager to Join 'Jihad' Against America," *USA Today*, September 27, 2001, p. 12. Six thousand of Pakistan's 40,000 madrassahs are militant. Though the schools, which are the primary means to an education for the poor of Pakistan, teach some mathematics and geography, their main staple is political and religious intolerance.
10. See Jeffrey Goldberg, "The Education of a Holy Warrior," *The New York Times Magazine,* June 25, 2000, pp. 32-37, 53, 63-64, 70-71.
11. The president's address to the nation can be found at http://www.georgebush.com.
12. For information on the decline of the Ottoman Empire and the effects of that collapse, see Jason Goodwin, *Lords of the Horizon: A History of the Ottoman Empire* (NY: Henry Holt and Company, 1998).
13. Armstrong, pp. 144-49.
14. "Deobandi Islam: The Religion of the Taliban." Information for this article was provided and used with permission from the Defense Language Institute at wrc.lingnet.org.
15. Bernard Lewis, "The Roots of Muslim Rage: Why so many Muslims deeply resent the West, and why their bitterness will not easily be mollified," *The Atlantic Online*, from the magazine's September 1990 edition , p. 16, www.theatlantic.com/issues/90sep/rage.htm.
16. Jonathan R. White, *Terrorism: An Introduction*, 3rd ed. (Belmont, CA: Wadsworth Thomson Learning, 2002), pp. 97-100. For fuller treatments, see David Fromkin, *A Peace to End All Peace: The Fall of the Ottoman Empire and the Creation of the Middle East* (NY: Avon Books, 1989); and A. J. Sherman, *Mandate Days: British Lives in Palestine, 1918–1948* (NY: Thames and Hudson, 1997).
17. Ibid., p. 55.
18. Lewis, "The Roots of Muslim Rage," p. 9.
19. Armstrong, p. 162.
20. For Middle East rates, see www.overpopulation.com. For U.S. results, see American Academy of Pediatrics Press Release, December 6, 1999, www.aap.org/advocacy/archives/decvital.htm.

21. Lewis, "The Revolt of Islam," p. 58.
22. Lewis, "The Roots of Muslim Rage," p. 17.
23. Akbar S. Ahmed. *Islam Today: A Short Introduction to the Muslim World* (London: I.B. Tauris Publishers, 1999), p. 226.

Chapter 2—Terrorism: What Is It?

1. Christopher C. Harmon, *Terrorism Today* (London: Frank C. Cass, 2000), p. xv.
2. Michael Phillip Carter, "The French Revolution: 'Jacobin Terror'" in *The Morality of Terrorism: Religious and Secular Justifications,* David C. Rapoport and Yonah Alexander, eds. (New York: Pergamon Press, 1982), p. 133.
3. Bruce Hoffman, *Inside Terrorism* (New York: Columbia University Press, 1998), p. 16.
4. Ibid., pp. 26-27.
5. Ibid., p. 27.
6. Ibid., pp. 27-28.
7. Ibid., p. 31.
8. Brian Jenkins, *The Study of Terrorism: Definitional Problems,* P-6563 (Santa Monica, CA: RAND Corporation, December 1980), p. 10.
9. Walter Laqueur, *The New Terrorism: Fanaticism and the Arms of Mass Destruction* (New York: Oxford University Press, 1999), p. 8.
10. Jessica Stern, *The Ultimate Terrorists* (Cambridge, MA: Harvard University Press, 1999), p. 11.
11. Hoffman, p. 43.
12. Title 22, U.S. Code, cited in United States Department of State, *Patterns of Global Terrorism 2000* (Washington, D.C.: Department of State, 2001), p. vi.
13. Federal Bureau of Investigation, from the Internet, http://www.fbi.gov/publisher/terror/terusa.html.
14. Harmon, p. 1.
15. Department of Defense, from the Internet, http://www.periscope.usni.com/demo/terms/t0000282.html.
16. Laqueur, pp. 210-11.
17. Ibid., pp. 211-12.
18. Ibid.
19. For a current summary of narcoterrorism, see Stephen Blank, "Narcoterrorism as a Threat to International Security," *The World & I,* December 2001, pp. 265-81.
20. Harmon, p. xv.
21. Ibid., p. 1.

Chapter 3—Terrorism's Trail of Tears

1. Robert Fisk, "We'll fight to the end, martyrdom is our victory," *The Independent* (UK), November 30, 2001, Internet edition (http://news.independent.co.uk/world/asia_china/story.jsp?story=107551).
2. Cited in Bruce Hoffman, *Inside Terrorism* (New York: Columbia University Press, 1998), p. 87.
3. Bruce Hoffman, "Holy Terror: The Implications of Terrorism Motivated by a Religious Imperative" (Santa Monica, CA: RAND Corp., 1994), p. 2; and Magnus Ranstrop, "Terrorism in the Name of Religion," *Journal of International Affairs* 50 (Summer 1996), pp. 45-46.
4. *De praescriptotione haereticorum,* 7.9.
5. David C. Rapoport, "Some General Observations on Religion and Violence," *Terrorism and Political Violence* 3:3 (Autumn 1991), p. 121.
6. Cited in Rapoport, p. 121.
7. Josephus, *The Wars of the Jews,* 7.10.2.
8. *Encyclopedia Judaica,* s.v. "Sicarii."

9. Josephus, 7.10.2.

10. Walter Lacqueur, *A History of Terrorism* (New Brunswick, NJ: Transaction Publishers, 2001), p. 8.

11. David C. Rapoport, "Fear and Trembling: Terrorism in Three Religious Traditions," *The American Political Science Review* 78:3 (September 1984), p. 664.

12. Bernard Lewis, *The Assassins: A Radical Sect in Islam* (New York: Oxford University Press, 1987), p. 134.

13. Lacqueur, pp. 8-9.

14. Rapoport, "Fear and Trembling," p. 665.

15. This is addressed further in chapter 4. See also Nasra Hassan's essay, "An Arsenal of Believers: Talking to the 'Human Bombs,'" *The New Yorker,* November 19, 2001, pp. 36-41.

16. Rapoport, "Fear and Trembling," p. 665.

17. Lewis, p. 140.

18. Rapoport, "Fear and Trembling," p. 662.

19. W. H. Sleeman, *Ramaseeana* (Calcutta: Huttman, 1836), p. 36, cited in Rapoport, "Fear and Trembling," p. 662.

20. Rapoport, "Fear and Trembling," p. 662.

21. W. H. Sleeman, *The Thugs or Phansigars of India* (Philadelphia: Carey and Hart, 1839), pp. 3-4, cited in Rapoport, "Fear and Trembling," p. 664.

22. Hoffman, "Holy Terror," p. 2.

23. James A. Haught, *Holy Hatred: Religious Conflicts of the '90s* (Amherst, NY: Prometheus Books, 1995), pp. 61-65.

24. Mark Juergensmeyer, *Terror in the Mind of God: The Global Rise of Religious Violence* (Berkeley: University of California Press, 2000), pp. 36-38.

25. W.B. Yeats, "Remorse for Intemperate Speech," in *The Collected Poems of W.B. Yeats,* ed. Richard J. Finneran, rev. second ed. (New York: Simon & Schuster, 1989), p. 254.

26. Cited in Jessica Stern, *The Ultimate Terrorists* (Cambridge, MA: Harvard University Press, 1999), p. 74.

27. Manabu Watanabe, "Religion and Violence in Japan Today: A Chronological and Doctrinal Analysis of Aum Shinrikyo," *Terrorism and Political Violence,* 10:4 (Winter 1998), p. 80.

28. Ibid.

29. William Rosenau, "Aum Shinrikyo's Biological Weapons Program: Why Did It Fail?" *Studies in Conflict & Terrorism* 24 (2001), p. 291.

30. Watanabe, p. 94.

31. Ibid., p. 95. See also Robert J. Lifton's *Destroying the World to Save It: Aum Shinrikyo, Apocalyptic Violence, and the New Global Terrorism* (New York: Metropolitan Books, 1999); and D.W. Brackett, *Holy Terror: Armageddon in Tokyo* (New York: Weatherhill, Inc., 1996).

32. Walter Laqueur, *The New Terrorism: Fanaticism and the Arms of Mass Destruction* (New York: Oxford University Press), p. 260.

33. For an extended treatment of the conflicts in this region, see Eric S. Margolis, *War at the Top of the World: The Struggle for Afghanistan, Kashmir, and Tibet* (New York: Routledge, 2000).

34. John F. Burns, "Kashmir's Islamic Guerillas See Little to Fear From U.S.," *New York Times,* December 24, 2001, p. A-1. See also Jonah Blank, "Kashmir: Fundamentalism Takes Root," *Foreign Affairs,* November-December, 1999, pp. 36-53.

35. Juergensmeyer, p. 208.

36. For an overview of Sikh history, religion, and politics, see Patwant Singh, *The Sikhs* (London: John Murray, 1999).

37. Caryle Murphy, "Bin Laden's Radical Form of Islam," *The Washington Post,* September 18, 2001, p. A-23.

38. For a good summary and overview of major terrorist groups around the world, see the U.S. State Department's annual publication *Patterns of Global Terrorism,* available on the Internet

at http://www.state.gov. See also the "Comprehensive List of Terrorists and Groups Identified Under Executive Order 13224" at the same site.

39. Bernard Lewis, "The Revolt of Islam," *The New Yorker,* November 19, 2001, p. 61.

40. Hoffman, *Inside Terrorism,* pp. 221-22, n. 18.

41. "Hezbollah: Identity and Goals" from the official website of Hezbollah, http://www.hizbullah.net/english/info.htm. Copied December 3, 2001.

42. Ibid.

43. Hoffman, *Inside Terrorism,* pp. 96-97.

44. Cited in Hoffman, *Inside Terrorism,* p. 97.

45. Nasra Hassan, "An Arsenal of Believers: Talking to the 'Human Bombs,'" *The New Yorker,* November 19, 2001, p. 39.

46. "The Spider in the Web: Osama bin Laden's Network," *The Economist,* September 22, 2001, p. 17.

47. Hassan, p. 38.

Chapter 4—Terrorism's Theology

1. Brad Hoffman, *Inside Terrorism* (New York: Columbia University Press, 1998), p. 94.

2. Mark Juergensmeyer, "Terror Mandated by God," *Terrorism and Political Violence* 9:2 (Summer 1997), p. 16.

3. Mark Juergensmeyer, "Sacrifice and Cosmic War," *Terrorism and Political Violence* 3:3 (Fall 1991), p. 102.

4. Ibid.

5. Juergensmeyer, "Terror Mandated by God," p. 19.

6. Ibid., p. 20.

7. Juergensmeyer, "Sacrifice and Cosmic War," p. 111.

8. Hoffman, pp. 92-94.

9. Ibid., p. 94.

10. Ibid.

11. Juergensmeyer, "Sacrifice and Cosmic War," p. 104.

12. Mark Juergensmeyer, "The Logic of Religious Violence," in David C. Rapoport, ed., *Inside Terrorist Organizations* (London: Frank Cass, 1988), pp. 185-90.

13. Juergensmeyer, "Sacrifice and Cosmic War," p. 111.

14. We are indebted to Hoffman's writings for these ideas and comparisons. See especially *Inside Terrorism,* pp. 94-96.

15. Cited in Mark Juergensmeyer, "The Terrorists Who Long for Peace," *The Fletcher Forum of World Affairs* 20:1 (Winter/Spring 1996), p. 2.

16. Cited in Hoffman, *Inside Terrorism,* p. 96.

17. Brad Hoffman, *Holy Terror: The Implications of Terrorism Motivated by a Religious Imperative* (Santa Monica, CA: RAND Corp., 1994), pp. 2-4.

18. David C. Rapoport, "Messianic Sanctions for Terror," *Comparative Politics* 20 (January 1988), pp. 197-98.

19. Cited in Sonia L. Alianak, "Religion, Politics, and Assassination in the Middle East: The Messianic Model," *World Affairs* 160:3 (Winter 1998), p. 163.

20. Juergensmeyer, "The Terrorists Who Long for Peace," p. 2.

21. A. Ezzati, "The Concept of Martyrdom in Islam," *Al-Serat* 12 (1986), Internet edition, http://www.al-islam.org/al-serat/Concept-Ezzati.htm.

22. Nasra Hassan, "An Arsenal of Believers: Talking to the 'Human Bombs,'" *The New Yorker,* November 19, 2001, p. 38. See also Ehud Sprinzak, "Rational Fanatics," *Foreign Policy,* September-October 2000, pp. 66-73; and Jeffrey Goldberg, "The Martyr Strategy," *The New Yorker,* July 9, 2001, pp. 34-39.

23. Hassan, p. 38.

24. Jessica Stern, *The Ultimate Terrorists* (Cambridge, MA: Harvard University Press, 1999), p. 49.
25. Cited in Stern, p. 87.
26. Juergensmeyer, "Terror Mandated by God," p. 22.
27. See for example, "Two Views: Can the Koran Condone Terror?" *The New York Times,* October 13, 2001, p. A-15.
28. Robert Worth, "The Deep Intellectual Roots of Islamic Terror," *The New York Times,* October 13, 2001, p. A-13. See also Bernard Lewis, "The Roots of Muslim Rage," *The Atlantic Monthly,* September 1990, Internet edition, http://www.theatlantic.com/issues/90sep/rage.htm; and "The Revolt of Islam," *The New Yorker,* November 19, 2001, pp. 50-63.
29. Rudoph Peters, *Jihad in Classical and Modern Islam* (Princeton, NJ: Markus Wiener Publishers, 1996), p. 1.
30. George W. Braswell, Jr., *Islam: Its Prophet, Peoples, Politics, and Power* (Nashville: Broadman & Holman Publishers, 1996), p. 71.
31. Peters, p. 3.
32. Ibid.
33. Akbar S. Ahmed, *Islam Today: A Short Introduction to the Muslim World* (London: I. B. Tauris Publishers, 1999), p. 8.
34. Bernard Lewis, "The Revolt of Islam," *The New Yorker,* November 19, 2001, p. 52.
35. Ibid. See also Braswell, p. 71.
36. Lewis, p. 60.
37. "Deobandi Islam: The Religion of the Taliban" (Monterey, CA: Defense Language Institute, n.d.), p. 3, taken from the Internet, http://www.wrc.lingnet.org.
38. For a good and balanced synopsis of politics, religion, and terrorism in the Middle East, see Jonathan R. White, *Terrorism: An Introduction,* 3rd ed. (Belmont, CA: Wadsworth Thomson Learning, 2002), pp. 91-111, 152-70.
39. Carl F. H. Henry, *Carl Henry at His Best* (Portland, OR: Multnomah Press, 1989), p. 114.

Chapter 5—Terrorism's Tactics, Targets, and Trends

1. Cited in Michael T. Osterholm and John Schwartz, *Living Terrors* (New York: Dell Publishing, 2000), p. xv.
2. Brian M. Jenkins, "Terrorism and Beyond: A 21st Century Perspective," *Studies in Conflict & Terrorism,* 24 (2001), pp. 324-25.
3. Brian M. Jenkins, "This Time Is Different," *San Diego Union Tribune,* September 16, 2001, taken from the Internet.
4. Ibid.
5. James F. Hogue, Jr., and Gideon Rose, eds., "Introduction," *How Did This Happen?: Terrorism and the New War* (New York: Council on Foreign Relations, 2001), p. x.
6. Cited in Karen DeYoung and Michael Dobbs, "Bin Laden: Architect of New Global Terrorism," *The Washington Post,* September 16, 2001, p. A-8.
7. Brian M. Jenkins, *International Terrorism: The Other World War,* R-3302-AF (Santa Monica, CA: RAND, November 1985), p. 12.
8. Ibid., p. 13.
9. Jenkins, "Terrorism and Beyond: A 21st Century Perspective," p. 323.
10. Brian M. Jenkins, "The Organization Men: Anatomy of a Terrorist Attack" in Hogue and Rose, p. 7.
11. Walter Laqueur, *The New Terrorism: Fanaticism and the Arms of Mass Destruction* (New York: Oxford University Press, 1999), p. 254.
12. Jonathan R. White, *Terrorism: An Introduction,* 3rd ed. (Belmont, CA: Wadsworth Thomson Learning, 2002), pp. 16-17.
13. Jenkins, *International Terrorism,* pp. 14–15.

14. Ibid., pp. 15-18.

15. Felicity Barringer, "New Tactics of Terrorists Is to Attack the Media," *New York Times,* October 15, 2001, pp. C-1, 13.

16. Jessica Stern, *The Ultimate Terrorists* (Cambridge, MA: Harvard University Press, 1999), p. 4.

17. Bruce Hoffman, *Inside Terrorism* (New York: Columbia University Press, 1998), p. 182.

18. Ibid., pp. 183-84.

19. Ibid., p. 184

20. Christopher C. Harmon, *Terrorism Today* (London: Frank Cass, 2000), p. 187.

21. Ibid., pp. 186-233. We have summarized Harmon's presentation, but the full presentation and significance should not be neglected. He provides some of the best ethical and philosophical critiques of terrorism we have found. See also his article "Terrorism: A Matter for Moral Judgment," *Terrorism and Political Violence* 4:1 (Spring 1992), pp. 1-21.

22. Ibid., p. 190.

23. Ibid.

24. Ibid., p. 191.

25. Ibid., p. 198.

26. Ibid.

27. Ibid., p. 200.

28. See Ben Barber, "Pakistan's Jihad Hatcheries," *The World & I,* December 2001, pp. 68-73.

29. Ibid., p. 208.

30. Ibid., p. 212.

31. Ibid., p. 217.

32. Eileen MacDonald, *Shoot the Women First* (New York: Random House, 1991), p. 235.

33. Ibid., p. 233.

34. Harmon, p. 190.

35. Samuel P. Huntington, *The Clash of Civilizations and the Remaking of World Order* (New York: Simon & Schuster, 1996), p. 21.

36. Ibid., p. 28.

37. For a fuller presentation of the ramifications of Huntington's model and war, see Demy's "Holy Hatred: The Return of Religious Nationalism and Future Global Conflict" in Timothy J. Demy and Gary P. Stewart, *Politics and Public Policy: A Christian Response* (Grand Rapids, MI: Kregel Publications, 2000), pp. 317-29.

38. See, for example, Stern, pp. 5-6.

39. Simon Reeve, *The New Jackals: Ramzi Yousef, Osama bin Laden and the Future of Terrorism* (Boston: Northeastern University Press, 1999), p. 257.

Chapter 6—Terrorism, the Taliban, and a Tangled Web

1. World Islamic Front Statement, "Jihad Against Jews and Crusaders," February 23, 1998, cited in Yonah Alexander and Michael S. Swetman, *Usama bin Laden's al-Qaida: Profile of a Terrorist Network* (Ardsley, NY: Transnational Publications, 2001), Appendix 1. This declaration is well publicized and available from many sources and Internet sites.

2. United States Department of State, *Patterns of Global Terrorism 2000* (Washington, D.C.: Department of State, 2000), p. 1. This is also available on the Internet at http://www.state.gov/ www/global/terrorism/index.html.

3. Professor Paul Wilkinson, chair of the Center for the Study of Terrorism and Political Violence, St. Andrews University, cited in Christopher C. Harmon, *Terrorism Today* (London: Frank Cass, 2000), p. 187.

4. Karen DeYoung and Michael Dobbs, "Bin Laden: Architect of New Global Terrorism," *The Washington Post,* September 16, 2001, p. A-8.

5. Peter L. Bergen, *Holy War, Inc.: Inside the Secret World of Osama bin Laden* (New York: The Free Press, 2001), p. 195. Bergen's work offers an enormous amount of information on the formal and informal aspects of bin Laden's network of terror.

6. DeYoung and Dobbs, p. A-8.

7. Cited in "Hate Club," *Time*, November 12, 2001, p. 65.

8. Marc Miller and Jason File, *Terrorism Factbook* (Peoria, IL: Bollix Books, 2001), p. 26.

9. "The Spider in the Web," *The Economist*, September 22, 2001, p. 17.

10. For more on the Palestinian issue, see Samuel R. Berger and Mona Suthpen, "Commandeering the Palestinian Cause: Bin Laden's Belated Cause" in James, F. Hoge, Jr., and Gideon Rose, eds. *How Did This Happen? Terrorism and the New War* (New York: Council on Foreign Relations, 2001), pp. 123-28.

11. DeYoung and Dobbs, p. A-8.

12. Yoni Fighel, "Sheikh Abdullah Azzam: Bin Laden's Spiritual Mentor," September 27, 2001, p. 2, taken from the Institute for Counter-Terrorism website, http://www.ict.org.il.

13. Miller and File, p. 28.

14. Philip P. Pan and John Pomfret, "Bin Laden's Chinese Connection," *The Washington Post*, November 10, 2001, p. A-10.

15. Bergen, p. 220.

16. Ahmed Rashid, *Taliban: Militant Islam, Oil and Fundamentalism in Central Asia* (New Haven: Yale University Press, 2000), p. 7. The Introduction in Rashid's volume provides a good synopsis of the long, rich, and violent history of Afghanistan.

17. See Jeffrey Meyers, "The Great Game and the Afghan Wars," *The World & I*, January 2002, pp. 271-83.

18. Cited in Ben MacIntyre, "The Bloodstained History of Afghanistan," *The Times* (London), October 5, 2001, Internet edition, http://www.thetimes.co.uk/article/0,,2001340009-2001344913,00.html. See also other articles from this same day in a series on the history of Afghanistan in *The Times*.

19. Ibid.

20. For a summary of the civil war, see Ali A. Jalali, "Afghanistan: The Anatomy of an Ongoing Conflict," *Parameters* 31:1 (Spring 2001), pp. 85-98. For a more in-depth history and analysis, see Larry P. Goodson, *Afghanistan's Endless War: State Failure, Regional Politics, and the Rise of the Taliban* (Seattle: University of Washington Press, 2001).

21. Robert D. Kaplan, "The Lawless Frontier," *The Atlantic Monthly*, September 2000, p. 72. This essay has also been added to the revised edition of Kaplan's 1990 work, *Soldiers of God: With Islamic Warriors in Afghanistan and Pakistan* (New York: Vintage Books, 2001).

22. Carl F. H. Henry, *Carl Henry at His Best* (Portland, OR: Multnomah Press, 1989), p. 100.

23. For a discussion of biblical views of government and Christian responsibility, see Dennis P. Hollinger, "The Purpose of Government: A Theological Perspective" and H. Wayne House, "What in the World Is the Church Supposed to Be Doing?" in *Politics and Public Policy: A Christian Response*, Timothy J. Demy and Gary P. Stewart, eds. (Grand Rapids: Kregel Publications, 2000), pp. 23-38 and 265-76, respectively.

24. Henry, p. 19.

Chapter 7—Technological Terror

1. Jon Swartz, "Experts Fear Cyberspace Could Be Terrorists' Next Target," *USA Today*, October 9, 2001, p. B-1.

2. Dave Kristula, "The History of the Internet," March 1997 with update in August 2001 at http://www.davesite.com/webstation/net-history.shtml. See also "PBS, Life on the Internet, Timeline" at http://www.pbs.org/internet/timeline/timeline-txt.html.

3. "PBS, Life on the Internet."

4. William J. Bayles, "The Ethics of Computer Network Attack," *Parameters* 31 (Spring 2001), Vol. 31, p. 57.

5. Matthew G. Devost, Brian K. Houghton, and Neal A. Pollard, "Information Terrorism: Can You Trust Your Toaster?," 1996, p. 10, at http://www.terrorism.com.

6. Stephen R. Bowers and Kimberly R. Keys, "Technology and Terrorism: The New Threat for the Millennium," *Conflict Studies* 309 (May 1998), p. 7.

7. Bruce Berkowitz, "Information Warfare: Time to Prepare," *The World & I*, January 2002, p. 148.

8. For this and other defacement activities, go to www.attrition.com. This website is dedicated to collecting examples of defacements that take place around the world.

9. For more illustrations see Dorothy Denning, "Cyberwarriors: Activists and Terrorists Turn to Cyberspace," *Harvard International Review*, Summer 2001, pp. 70-75.

10. Richard Forno, "Code Red Is Not the Problem," at http://www.infowarrior.org/articles/2001-07.html, August 5, 2000. For a complete discussion of Microsoft's software problems, see Richard Forno, "Microsoft: A Proven Danger to National Security," at www.infowarrior.com, May 15, 2000, 21 pages.

11. WebSTAR press release, "WebSTAR Server Suite Recruited by the U.S. Army for Greater Web Security," September 14, 1999. See http://www.webstar.com/press/press-releases/pr091499.html.

12. Chris Taylor, "Why Worms Like Code Red Are Good for You," at http://www.time.com/time/columnist/taylor/article/0,9565,169678,00.html, August 1, 2001.

13. Jessica Eve Stern, "The Covenant, the Sword, and the Arm of the Lord," *Toxic Terror: Assessing Terrorist Use of Chemical and Biological Weapons* (Cambridge, MA: MIT Press, 2001), pp. 156, 285.

14. Adam Cohen, "When Terror Hides Online," *Time*, November 12, 2001, p. 65.

15. Denning, p. 70.

16. "Patterns of Global Terrorism," U.S. Department of State, Washington, D.C., April 2001. "Terrorists have seized upon the worldwide practice of using information technology (IT) in daily life. They embrace IT for several reasons: it improves communication and aids organization, allows members to coordinate quickly with large numbers of followers, and provides a platform for propaganda. The Internet also allows terrorists to reach a wide audience of potential donors and recruits who may be located over a large geographic area," p. 36. See also John Schwartz, "Securing the Lines of a Wired Nation," *The New York Times*, October 4, 2001, p. F-4.

17. Press release, United States Department of Justice, "Juvenile Computer Hacker Cuts off FAA Tower: At Regional Airport—First Federal Charges Brought Against a Juvenile for Computer Crime," March 18, 1998. See http://www.usdoj.gov/criminal/cybercrime/juvenilepld.htm. This story recounts a 1997 hacker incident in Worchester, Massachusetts, which may have awakened authorities to the possibility of an electronic terrorist attack against an airport. A teenager identified the telephone numbers of the modems connected to the loop carrier systems of the phone company that served the airport. After connecting to the telephone company's computer system through his PC's modem, he sent a series of commands that corrupted the integrity of the data upon which the system relied, successfully disabling phone service. Telephone service to the tower at the airport, the airport fire department and security, the weather service, and private airfreight companies was lost for more than six hours. The greatest danger came from the loss of power to a main radio transmitter and a circuit that enabled aircraft to remotely activate the runway's approach lights. Fortunately there was no catastrophe.

18. Berkowitz, p. 150.

19. Ibid.

20. Robert J. Bunker, "Weapons of Mass Destruction and Terrorism," *Terrorism and Public Violence*, 12:1 (Spring 2000), p. 40.

21. Bill Wallace, "Next Major Attack Could Be over Net, Power Grids, 911 Shown to Be Vulnerable," *The San Francisco Chronicle*, November 12, 2001.

22. Ibid.

23. Richard Forno, "September 11th Does Not Mean Cyberwar Is Coming," at http://www.infowarrior.org/articles/2001-08.html, September 13, 2001.

24. Peter Carbonara, "Dirty Money," *Money*, January 2002, p. 91.

Chapter 8—Toxic Terror

1. Vannevar Bush, *Modern Arms and Free Men* (New York: Simon and Schuster, 1949), p. 142. Cited in Donald C. Hickman, "Biological Warfare and American Strategic Risk." A thesis presented to the faculty of the School of Advanced Airpower Studies, Air University, Maxwell Air Force Base, Alabama, June 2000, p. 3.

2. Time/CNN Poll conducted on September 27, 2001 in *Time*, October 8, 2001, pp. 28-29.

3. Jeffrey K. Smart, "Chapter 2, History of Chemical and Biological Warfare: An American Perspective" in *Textbook of Military Medicine: Medical Aspects of Chemical and Biological Warfare*, Brigadier General Russ Zajtchuk, U.S.A., and Colonel Ronald F. Bellamy, U.S.A., eds. (Office of the Surgeon General, Department of the Army, United States of America, 1997), pp. 25-36. USAMRIID, "History of Biological Warfare: Significant Events," http://usamriid. army.mil/content/BioWarCourse/HISTORY/HISTORY.html. See also Donald C. Hickman, "Biological Warfare and American Strategic Risk," pp. 42-43. For more information, see Edward M. Eitzen, Jr., and Ernest T. Takafuji, "Historical Overview of Biological Warfare" in *Textbook of Military Medicine*.

4. See http://library.thinkquest.org/27393/dreamwvr/agents/mustard1.htm.

5. David Bjerklie, Christine Gorman, and Alice Park, "Diagnosing the Risks," *Time*, October 8, 2001, p. 44.

6. Jonathan B. Tucker, "Lessons from the Case Studies," in *Toxic Terror: Assessing Terrorist Use of Chemical and Biological Weapons*, Jonathan B. Tucker ed. (Cambridge, MA: MIT Press, 2001, third printing), p. 267.

7. John V. Parachini, "Comparing Motives and Outcomes of Mass Casualty Terrorism Involving Conventional and Unconventional Weapons," in *Studies in Conflict & Terrorism, 2001*, 24, p. 402.

8. R. Nicholas Palarino in a briefing memorandum, dated July 18, 2001, to the members of the subcommittee on National Security, Veteran Affairs, and International Relations for a hearing on "Combating Terrorism: Federal Response to a Biological Weapons Attack" slated for July 23, 2001, unnumbered introduction.

9. Adam Rodgers, Michael Isikoff, Daniel Klaidman, and Debra Rosenberg, "Assessing the Threat of 'Bugs' and 'Gas,'" *Newsweek*, October 8, 2001, p. 22.

10. Cited in Judith Miller, Stephen Engelberg, and William Board, *Germs: Biological Weapons and America's Secret War* (New York: Simon & Schuster, 2001), p. 163.

11. Ken Alibek, *Biohazard: The Chilling True Story of the Largest Covert Biological Weapons Program in the World—Told from Inside by the Man Who Ran It* (New York: Dell Publishing, 1999), p. xi.

12. See http://www.geocites.com/CapeCanaveral/Lab/7050/introduction.html.

13. U.S. Army, "Biological Agent Information Paper," on a CD entitled *21st Century Complete Guide to Bioterrorism, Biological and Chemical Weapons, Germs and Germ Warfare, Nuclear and Radiological Terrorism: Military Manuals and Federal Documents with Practical Emergency Plans, Protective Measures, Medical Treatment and Survival Information*. Document 02_14 on the introduction page. See also Ken Alibek, *Biohazard*, p. 167.

14. Alibek, p. 166.

15. No author, "Types of Biological Weapons," on abcnews.com at http://abcnews.go.com/sections/living/DailyNews/wtc_bioweapons.html, p. 2.

16. Alibek, p. 281.

17. Hickman, p. 15.

18. Alibek, pp. 258-62. Sergei Popov, who defected from Russia to Britain in 1992, was involved in bioweapons experimentation in the Soviet Union. "Rather than combining pathogens into unnatural hybrids or inserting foreign genes into microbes so as to express new toxins, he looked for ways to trigger autoimmune responses. The aim was to trick the body's defenses into self-destruction, as happens slowly in diseases like lupus and rheumatoid arthritis. 'Sometimes just small, very tiny quantities of foreign substances are enough,' he said 'to make the immune response quite devastating.'" Judith Miller et al., *Germs*, p. 301.

19. Hickman, pp. 29, 32.

20. Frank J. Cilluffo, Sharon L. Cardash, and Gordon N. Lederman, eds., *Combating Chemical, Biological, Radiological, and Nuclear Terrorism: A Comprehensive Study, A Report of the CSIS Homeland Defense Project* (Washington, D.C.: The Center for Strategic and International Studies Press, 2001), p. 2.

21. A statement made by William H. Webster in Ernest T. Takafuji and Allart B. Kok "The Chemical Warfare Threat and the Military Healthcare Provider," in *Textbook of Military Medicine: Medical Aspects of Chemical and Biological Warfare*, p. 154. Originally quoted in G. Browder, *Countering the Chemical and Biological Weapons Threat in the Post-Soviet World*. A report of the special inquiry into the chemical and biological threat of the Committee on Armed Services, U.S. House of Representatives, 102nd Congress (Washington, D.C.: U.S. Government Printing Office, February 23, 1993), p. 9.

22. Jonathan B. Tucker, "Introduction," in *Toxic Terror: Assessing Terrorist Use of Chemical and Biological Weapons*, p. 3.

23. No author, *Chem-Bio: Frequently Asked Questions, A Guide to Better Understanding Chem-Bio* (Alexandria, VA: Tempest Publishing, 1998), pp. 74-86. See also http://www.chem-bio. com.

24. Tucker, p. 5.

25. Takafuji and Kok, pp. 148-53.

26. Frederick R. Sidell, "Chemical Agent Terrorism," on a CD entitled *21st Century Complete Guide to Bioterrorism, Biological and Chemical Weapons, Germs and Germ Warfare, Nuclear and Radiological Terrorism*. Document 03_18, p. 3. Ernest T. Takafuji and Allart B. Kok, "The Chemical Warfare Threat," p. 155.

27. No Author given; "Sarin Nerve Gas" at http://www.geocites.com/CapeCanaveral/Lab/7050.

28. Sidell, pp. 1-2; and Joe Lenthall, "VX Gas," http://www.chem.ox.ac.uk/mom/vx/VX.htm.

29. Terence Nelan, "Iraq's Deadly Little Secret," at abcnews.com, November 14, 2001. See http://more.abcnews.go.com/sections/world/iraq1114_vx/.

30. Sidell, pp. 3-4; and Takafuji and Kok, pp. 155-56.

Chapter 9—Thinking the Unthinkable

1. Brian M. Jenkins, *Will Terrorists Go Nuclear?* (Santa Monica, CA: RAND Corporation, P-5541, November 1975), p. 7.

2. "Perspectives" *Newsweek*, December 10, 2001, p. 23.

3. *The Economist*, cited in Glenn E. Schweitzer with Carole C. Dorsch, *Superterrorism: Assassins, Mobsters, and Weapons of Mass Destruction* (New York: Plenum Trade, 1998), p. 51.

4. Cited in Simon Reeve, *The New Jackals: Ramzi Yousef, Osama bin Laden and the Future of Terrorism* (Boston: Northeastern University Press, 1999), p. v.

5. Three militia groups have been arrested since the 1995 bombing of the Alfred P. Murrah Building in Oklahoma City. In November 1995, members of the West Virginia Mountaineer Militia were arrested and charged with plotting to blow up an FBI computer center; in July of 1996, members of an Arizona group (Viper Militia) planning to blow up several federal buildings in Phoenix were charged with possession of explosives and conspiracy to promote civil disorder; later in 1996, three members of the Militia-At-Large for the Republic of Georgia were

arrested for planning to wage war with the United States government. For more information on America's radical militia groups, see Bruce Hoffman, *Inside Terrorism* (NY: Columbia University Press, 1998), pp. 105-20; and Richard Abanes, *American Militias: Rebellion, Racism & Religion* (Downers Grove, IL: InterVarsity Press, 1996).

6. Guy Gugliotta, "Technology of 'Dirty Bomb' Simple, but Not the Execution," *The Washington Post*, December 5, 2001, p. A-12.

7. David E. Kaplan and Douglas Pasternak, "Terror's Dirty Secret," *U.S. News & World Report*, December 3, 2001, pp. 27-28.

8. Abel Gonzalez, International Atomic Energy Agency's director of radiation and waste safety, cited by Sonya Yee, "Nuclear experts warn of threat from 'dirty bombs,'" *The Christian Science Monitor*, November 5, 2001, taken from the Internet.

9. Joseph B. Verrengia, "'Dirty bomb' scenario revives nuclear worries: Experts quickly refine their response plans for radiological terror attack," at http://www.msnbc.com/news/674098. asp?cpl=1, December 18, 2001.

10. Jessica Stern, *The Ultimate Terrorists* (Cambridge, MA: Harvard University Press, 1999), p. 56.

11. Reeve, p. 214.

12. Stern, pp. 52, 90.

13. Reeve, pp. 215-16.

14. Walter Laqueur, *The New Terrorism: Fanaticism and the Arms of Mass Destruction* (New York: Oxford University Press, 1999), p. 221. For an excellent discussion on the rise and power of organized crime in Russia and its connection to terrorism, see pages 218-25.

15. Stern, p. 88. For a thorough discussion on the condition in Russia from a political, military, and economic perspective, see pp. 87-106.

16. No author, "Russia Says It Foiled Illegal Sale of Weapons-Grade Uranium," *The New York Times*, December 7, 2001, p. A-8.

17. Bruce G. Blair, "The Ultimate Hatred Is Nuclear," *The New York Times*, October 22, 2001, p. A-21.

18. Ken Alibek, *Biohazard: The Chilling True Story of the Largest Covert Biological Weapons Program in the World—Told from Inside by the Man Who Ran It* (New York: Dell Publishing, 1999), p. 292.

19. Gregg Easterbrook, "The Big One: The Real Danger Is Nuclear," *The New Republic*, November 5, 2001, p. 25.

20. Reeve, p. 214.

Chapter 10—Targeting Terrorism Justly

1. Cited in Edward E. Ericson, Jr., "Alexandr Solzhenitsyn," *Christianity Today Online*, http://www.christianitytoday.com/ch/2000/001/7.32.html.

2. Arthur F. Holmes, "The Just War," in *War: Four Christian Views*, Robert G. Clouse, ed. (Downers Grove, IL: InterVarsity Press, 1991), p. 117.

3. Ibid., pp. 118-20. For issues of contemporary just war theory see Richard J. Regan, *Just War: Principles and Cases* (Washington, D.C.: The Catholic University Press of America, 1996).

4. Ibid., p. 118.

5. Dan Smith, *The State of War and Peace Atlas* (New York: The Penguin Group, 1997), p. 13.

6. Ibid.

7. Ibid., p. 14.

8. C. S. Lewis, *God in the Dock: Essays on Theology and Ethics,* Walter Hooper, ed. (Grand Rapids, MI: Eerdmans, 1970), p. 326.

9. Christopher C. Harmon, *Terrorism Today* (London: Frank Cass, 2000), p. 190.

10. James Turner Johnson, "In Response to Terror," *First Things* 90 (February 1999), p. 12.

11. Christopher C. Harmon, "Terrorism: A Matter for Moral Judgment," *Terrorism and Political Violence* 4:1 (Spring 1992), p. 17.

12. Johnson, p. 13.
13. Ibid.
14. Carl von Clausewitz, *On War*, Michael Howard and Peter Paret, eds. (Princeton, NJ: Princeton University Press, 1976), p. 80.
15. Harmon, *Terrorism Today*, p. 14.
16. C. S. Lewis, "Learning in Wartime" in *The Weight of Glory and Other Addresses,* orig. pub. New York: The Macmillan Company, paper edition (Grand Rapids: William B. Eerdmans, 1965), p. 44.

Chapter 11—Truth in Turbulent Times

1. William J. Bennett, *The Death of Outrage: Bill Clinton and the Assault on American Ideals* (New York: The Free Press, 1998), p. 40.
2. Carl F. H. Henry, *Carl Henry at His Best: A Lifetime of Quotable Thoughts* (Portland, OR: Multnomah, 1989), p. 143.
3. Ibid., p. 205.
4. Dennis P. Hollinger, "Terrorism Through the Eyes of Faith," *Knowing & Doing* (Winter 2001), p. 15.
5. Ibid., p. 15.
6. Paul Marshall, "Keeping the Faith: Religion, Freedom, and International Affairs," in Timothy J. Demy and Gary P. Stewart, eds., *Politics and Public Policy, A Christian Response: Crucial Considerations for Governing Life* (Grand Rapids, MI: Kregel Publications, 2000), pp. 289, 294. "The predominantly Christian population in southern Sudan is subject to torture, rape, and starvation for its refusal to convert to Islam. Christian children are routinely sold into slavery. Muslims who dare to convert to Christianity are faced with the death penalty" (p. 289).
7. Hollinger, p. 19.
8. For a wealth of quotes, see http://www.curiousquotes.com.
9. Wayne Grudem, *Systematic Theology: An Introduction to Biblical Doctrine* (Grand Rapids, MI: Zondervan, 1994), pp. 203-07. For a specific theological response to the events of September 11, see Robert Pyne, *What Can We Say About Evil in Light of America's Tragedy?* (Dallas: Dallas Theological Seminary, 2001).
10. See on the Internet http://www.curiousquotes.com.
11. O. Michel, "μισέω" in Gerhard Kittel, ed., *Theological Dictionary of the New Testament, volume IV, Λ–N* (Grand Rapids, MI: Wm. B. Eerdmans Publishing Company, 1967), p. 686.
12. Hollinger, pp. 12-13.
13. Thomas L. Friedman, "The Real War," *The New York Times*, November 27, 2001.

Chapter 12—Triumph over Tragedy

1. "The Day the World Changed," *The Economist,* September 15, 2001, p. 13.
2. Gene Edward Veith, "Reality in the Rubble," *World,* October 13, 2001, p. 13.
3. Ibid.
4. Ibid.
5. For good Christian critiques of postmodernism see J. Richard Middleton and Brian J. Walsh, *Truth Is Stranger Than It Used to Be: Biblical Faith in a Postmodern Age* (Downers Grove, IL: InterVarsity Press, 1995); and Paul Copan, *"True for You, But Not for Me": Deflating the Slogans that Leave Christians Speechless* (Minneapolis, MN: Bethany House Publishers, 1998).
6. Lance Morrow, "Awfully Ordinary," *Time,* December 24, 2001, p. 106.
7. C. S. Lewis, *Mere Christianity* (New York: Simon & Schuster, 1966 edition), p. 50.
8. Andree Seu, "True Perspectives," *World,* October 20, 2001, p. 41.
9. Brian M. Jenkins, "Terrorism and Beyond: A 21st Century Perspective," *Studies in Conflict & Terrorism* 24 (2001), pp. 326-27.
10. Carl F. H. Henry, *Gods of This Age or...God of the Ages?* (Nashville: Broadman & Holman Publishers, 1994), p. 291.
11. Mark Galli, "Now What?" *Christianity Today,* October 22, 2001, p. 27.

Recommended Reading

The resources listed below are among the many works cited in the endnotes and are recommended for those who want to pursue the issues we discussed. Inclusion in this list does not necessarily imply complete agreement with the contents of the titles, nor are all of the works in the endnotes cited.

Alibek, Ken, with Handelman, Stephen. *Biohazard.* New York: Random House, 1999.

Braswell, George W., Jr. *Islam: Its Prophet, People, Politics and Power.* Nashville: Broadman and Holman Publishers, 1996.

Bergen, Peter L. *Holy War, Inc.: Inside the Secret World of Osama bin Laden.* New York: The Free Press, 2001.

Emerson, Steven. American Jihad: *The Terrorists Living Among Us.* New York: The Free Press, 2002.

Harmon, Christopher C. *Terrorism Today.* London: Frank Cass, 2000.

Hoffman, Bruce. *Inside Terrorism.* New York: Columbia University Press, 1998.

Hogue, James F., Jr., and Rose, Gideon. *How Did This Happen?* New York: Council on Foreign Relations, 2001.

Juergensmeyer, Mark. *Terror in the Mind of God: The Global Rise of Religious Violence.* Berkeley, CA: University of California Press, 2000.

Kaplan, Robert D. *Soldiers of God: With Islamic Warriors in Afghanistan and Pakistan.* Rev. ed. New York: Vintage Books, 2001.

Laqueur, Walter. *The New Terrorism: Fanaticism and the Arms of Mass Destruction.* New York: Oxford University Press, 1999.

Lewis, Bernard. *Islam and the West.* New York: Oxford University Press, 1993.

———. "The Roots of Muslim Rage." *Atlantic Monthly,* September 1990, pp. 47-60.

———. "The Revolt of Islam." *The New Yorker,* November 21, 2001, pp. 50-63.

———. *What Went Wrong?: Western Impact and Middle Eastern Response.* New York: Oxford University Press, 2002.

Parshall, Phil. *Inside the Community: Understanding Muslims Through Their Traditions.* Grand Rapids, MI: Baker Books, 1994.

Price, Randall. *Unholy War: America, Israel, and Radical Islam.* Eugene, OR: Harvest House Publishers, 2001.

Reeve, Simon. *The New Jackals: Ramzi Yousef, Osama bin Laden and the Future of Terrorism.* Boston: Northeastern University Press, 1999.

Regan, Richard J. *Just War: Principles and Cases.* Washington, D.C.: The Catholic University Press of America, 1996.

Stern, Jessica. *The Ultimate Terrorists.* Cambridge, MA: Harvard University Press, 1999.

About the Authors

Timothy J. Demy is a military chaplain and has taught for six years as an adjunct instructor at the U.S. Naval War College, Newport, Rhode Island. He has served for more than 20 years in a variety of assignments with the U.S. Navy, U.S. Coast Guard, and U.S. Marine Corps. He is the coauthor and coeditor of more than two dozen books and has contributed to numerous journals, reference works, and books on social issues, ethics, and theology.

In addition to his theological training, which he received at Dallas Theological Seminary (Th.M., Th.D.), he holds graduate degrees in European history, human development, and national security and strategic studies. He was the President's Honor Graduate from the U.S. Naval War College and is currently a Ph.D. candidate at Salve Regina University, where he is studying technology and the humanities. He is a member of the Evangelical Theological Society, The Center for Bioethics and Human Dignity, and the Organization of American Historians. He has been listed in *Who's Who in America* and other similar volumes for several years and his work on religiously motivated terrorism has been used by the U.S. Navy and U.S. Marine Corps. He and his wife, Lyn, have been married 24 years.

Gary P. Stewart has been a military chaplain for more than 15 years and is presently serving with the U.S. Marine Corps. He has served previously with the U.S. Navy in several assignments and with the U.S. Coast Guard. He is the coauthor and coeditor of 12 volumes and has written numerous other articles in books, journals, and magazines. Gary has earned degrees from Trinity Graduate School (M.A. in Bioethics), Grace Theological Seminary (M.Div.), Bethel Theological Seminary (Th.M.), and Western Theological Seminary (D.Min.). He is presently a Ph.D. candidate at the University of Wales at Lampeter in the United Kingdom. He has studied broadly in the fields of theology, bioethics, and political science, and has lectured widely. He is a member of the Evangelical Theological Society and The Center for Bioethics and Human Dignity and is listed in *Who's Who in America*. His hobbies include woodworking and music. Gary and his wife, Kathie, have been married 25 years. They have two daughters, Lindsay Anne, who is married to Jeff, and Katie Anne. They have one granddaughter, Lauralyn.